MW01145970

I Want You to Be Happy

FINDING PEACE AND ABUNDANCE IN EVERYDAY LIFE

—

POPE FRANCIS

Translated from the Italian by
Oonagh Stransky

New York   Nashville

Copyright © FullDay srl 2023
Copyright © Libreria Editrice Vaticana-Dicastero di Communicazione 2023
Translation Copyright © 2025 Oonagh Stransky
Cover design by Faceout Studio. Cover copyright © 2024
by Hachette Book Group, Inc.

Hachette Book Group supports the right to free expression and the
value of copyright. The purpose of copyright is to encourage writers
and artists to produce the creative works that enrich our culture.

The scanning, uploading, and distribution of this book without
permission is a theft of the author's intellectual property. If you
would like permission to use material from the book (other than
for review purposes), please contact permissions@hbgusa.com.
Thank you for your support of the author's rights.

FaithWords
Hachette Book Group
1290 Avenue of the Americas, New York, NY 10104
faithwords.com
@FaithWords / @FaithWordsBooks

First published in Great Britain in 2024 by Hodder
& Stoughton, a Hachette UK company.

First Edition: February 2025

FaithWords is a division of Hachette Book Group, Inc. The FaithWords
name and logo are registered trademarks of Hachette Book Group, Inc.

The publisher is not responsible for websites (or their
content) that are not owned by the publisher.

The Hachette Speakers Bureau provides a wide range of authors for
speaking events. To find out more, go to hachettespeakersbureau.com
or email HachetteSpeakers@hbgusa.com.

FaithWords books may be purchased in bulk for business,
educational, or promotional use. For information, please contact
your local bookseller or the Hachette Book Group Special
Markets Department at special.markets@hbgusa.com.

All Scripture quotations are taken from the Holy Bible, New
International Version®, NIV®. Copyright ©1973, 1978, 1984,
2011 by Biblica, Inc.™ Used by permission of Zondervan. All
rights reserved worldwide. www.zondervan.com. The "NIV" and
"New International Version" are trademarks registered in the
United States Patent and Trademark Office by Biblica, Inc.™

Library of Congress Control Number: 2024945350

ISBNs: 9781546007975 (hardcover), 9781546007999 (ebook)

Printed in the United States of America

LSC-C

Printing 1, 2024

Contents

Introduction

"What Jesus did here in Cana of Galilee was the first of the signs through which he revealed his glory; and his disciples believed in him" (John 2:11). These are the final words from the Gospel of John about the story of the wedding at Cana, when Jesus transforms water into wine for the bride and groom. John the Evangelist does not mention a miracle, there is no powerful and extraordinary deed that brings about wonder; he writes that a *sign* took place at Cana, one that sparked the faith of his disciples.

What is a "sign" in the context of the Gospel? A sign is a clue that reveals God's love. It does not call our attention to the power of the action, but to the love that exists behind it. It teaches us something about God's love, how it is always near, tender and compassionate.

This sign, which is also Jesus' first, occurs when the couple suddenly find themselves in difficulty on the most important day of their lives. Right in the middle of the feast, there is a shortage of wine, one of the key elements of the festivity; if it were to run out, the celebration might end and the guests would go away unhappy. A wedding party can hardly continue just with water!

It is actually Mary who realizes that there is a problem; she is the one who discreetly brings it to Jesus' attention, and he intervenes without any fanfare. It all takes place very quietly, behind the scenes. This is precisely how God operates—with thoughtfulness and discretion. In fact, all the compliments from the guests on the quality of the wine go to the bridegroom.

How truly glorious it is that Jesus' first sign was not an extraordinary healing or a miracle that unfolded in the Temple of Jerusalem, but an act that responded to a simple and practical need of ordinary people: it was a domestic gesture and it was performed "on tiptoes," in silence.

But the sign that took place in Cana is important for another reason. Usually, the wine served toward the end of a feast would be of a lesser quality—by that point, the guests would not notice if it had even been watered down a little. Jesus, on the other hand, makes sure that the feast ends with *the best wine*. Symbolically, this tells us that God wants what is best for us: he wants us to be happy.

God does not set limits on us and he does not demand interest. He has no ulterior motives or expectations. The joy that Jesus leaves in our hearts is complete and selfless. It is never a watered-down kind of joy. It is a joy that constantly renews us.

"I am making everything new!" This is the word of God in the book of Revelation (21:5). Our God is the God of newness. He is the God of surprises. He brings freshness into the life of humankind; he creates change in both history and the cosmos. God consistently creates new things, and he asks us to look kindly on novelty: new wine in new wineskins.

It is not Christian to walk with one's gaze directed at the ground, to walk without raising one's eyes up to the horizon, as if our entire journey covered only a few meters, as if our life had no goal or mooring, as if we were compelled to wander endlessly and without reason for our many troubles.

This is not Christian.

We are not alive by mistake; God desired life for us. He created us because he wants us to be happy. He is our Father, and if our lives in the here and now are not what he wanted for us, Jesus assures us that God is working to redeem us.

Being Christians means having a new perspective, and looking at things with hope. We believe and know that death and hate are not the final words on the parabola of human existence.

Some people believe that we only know happiness when we are young, that it is bound up in the past, that life is actually slow deterioration. Others think that any kind of joy we experience is fleeting and momentary, that human life is meaningless.

But we Christians do not think that. No, we believe that resting on the horizon of life is a sun that shines forever. We believe that our most beautiful days are yet to come. We are people of the spring, as opposed to the autumn. Let us look to the buds of a new world rather than yellowed leaves on its branches.

A Christian knows that the kingdom of God, the dominion of Love, grows like a vast field of wheat, and that it may well have weeds in its midst. There are always problems: people gossip, there are wars, there is illness...But even so, the wheat ripens, and in the end evil will be eliminated.

We know that the future does not belong to us. We know that Jesus Christ is life's greatest grace. We know that God's warm embrace not only awaits us at life's end but also accompanies us on our journey every day.

Let us not cultivate nostalgia, regret and sorrow. God wants us to be the heirs of a promise; he wants us to be tireless growers of dreams.

Fifteen Steps Toward Happiness

1. *Read the book of your life story.* Our life is the most precious book we have been given; it holds that which we seek elsewhere in vain. St. Augustine understood this: "Return to yourself. In our interior, the truth resides."[1] I extend this invitation to all of you—and even to myself: read your life story. Look within, ask yourself how your journey has been. Do it with serenity. Return within.

2. *Remember that you are unique.* We all are. We were brought into this world to be loved for who we are and to love others in our own unique and special way. Life is not a game where we sit on the sidelines, waiting to be called in as a substitute for someone else. No: each of us is unique in God's eyes. Don't let yourself be "standardized." None of us is standard issue; we are all unique, free and alive, called on to live out a love story with God, to make bold and firm decisions, to accept the marvelous risk of loving.

3. *Allow your beauty to shine!* I am not talking about the kind of beauty that is shaped by fashion, but true beauty. Not the kind of beauty that leads a person to focus solely on themselves, like Narcissus in Greek mythology, who fell in love with his reflection in a pool of water and then drowned in it. Not the kind of beauty that strikes a deal with evil, like Dorian Gray, who, when the spell ended,

found himself with a disfigured face.[2] I am talking about the kind of beauty that never fades because it is a reflection of *divine* beauty. Our God is simultaneously good, true and beautiful. And beauty is one of the special ways we can reach him.

4. *Learn to laugh at yourself.* Narcissists constantly look in the mirror...I suggest that every so often you look in the mirror and laugh at yourself. Laugh at yourself! It will do you good.

5. *Be wholesomely restless.* In your projects and dreams, experience the kind of restlessness that will encourage you to keep moving forward, never feeling as though you have "arrived." Do not cut yourself off from the world by locking yourself in your room—like a Peter Pan who never wants to grow up—but be open and courageous.

6. *Learn to forgive.* Everyone knows they are not the father or mother they should be; they are not the bride or groom, the brother or sister or friend they should be. We all have flaws. And we all need mercy. Remember that we all need to forgive; we need forgiveness and we need patience. And remember that God precedes us in everything. He is always the first to forgive.

7. *Learn to read sadness.* In our day and age, sadness is generally seen as something negative, an ill to avoid at all costs. Instead, sadness can be a valuable alarm, inviting us to explore richer and more fertile landscapes precluded by superficiality and escapism. Sometimes sadness works like a red traffic signal: Stop! Welcome that signal into your life; it will be much worse if you choose to ignore it.

8. *Dream big.* Do not settle for merely what you feel you are owed in life. The Lord doesn't want us to limit our horizons; he doesn't want us to sit in a parked car by the side of the road. He wants us to rush toward higher goals with joy and audacity. We were not created just to dream about holidays and weekends, but to make our godly dreams in this life come true. He made us capable of dreaming so we can embrace the beauty of life.

9. *Don't listen to people who peddle illusions.* Dreaming is one thing; having illusions is something else. Those who speak about dreams but peddle illusions are trying to manipulate your happiness. We were created for a greater kind of joy.

10. *Be revolutionary and go against the grain.* In our unstable and often ephemeral world, there are people who try to preach the importance of "enjoying" the moment. They say it is not worth making a lifelong commitment to something, that it is not good to make strong decisions because we do not know what tomorrow will bring. I ask you to be a revolutionary and to rebel against this culture, which, underneath it all, would have you believe that you are incapable of assuming your responsibilities. Have the courage to be happy.

11. *Take risks, even if it means making mistakes.* Don't watch life pass by from a balcony. Don't confuse happiness with a sofa. Let your dreams flower and make strong decisions. Take risks. Don't go through life anesthetized or approach the world like a tourist. Make some noise! Cast out the fears that paralyze you. Live! Live life fully and in the best way possible!

12. *Walk with others*. It is terrible to walk alone: terrible and tedious. By walking with others, with friends, with those who love us, we help ourselves reach our goals. And if you fall, get back on your feet. Do not be afraid of failure, of falling. In the art of walking, what is important is not to stay down.

13. *Live gratuitously*. The lives of people who do not give freely of themselves become a kind of frenetic commerce, where we constantly measure what we give and what we receive. God gives freely, even helping those who are unfaithful. "He causes his sun to rise on the evil and the good" (Matt. 5:45). We received life freely; we paid nothing for it. Consequently, all of us can give without expecting anything in return. This is what Jesus told his disciples: "Freely you have received; freely give" (Matt. 10:8). This is the meaning of a full life.

14. *Look beyond the darkness*. Make the effort to find light even in the darkness. We must never stop seeking the light in whatever darkness may be in our hearts or around us. Lift up your gaze from earth to heaven, not to flee but to resist the temptation to remain imprisoned by your fears. The danger is that our fears will overrule us, that we will remain closed in on ourselves and cry and complain. Look toward heaven!

15. *Remember that you are destined for great things*. God wants the best for us; he wants us to be happy. He does not set limits and he does not charge us interest. Jesus is by our side; there are no ulterior motives or expectations. The joy he leaves in our hearts is complete and selfless. It is never watered down, but constantly renewed.

PART I

HAPPINESS IS A GIFT
WE RECEIVE

ONLY LOVE CAN BRING
HAPPINESS INTO OUR LIVES

"For whoever wants to save their life will lose it, but whoever loses their life for me will find it" (Matt. 16:25). This paradox contains the golden rule that God inscribed in the human nature created in Christ: only love can give meaning and happiness to life. Spending your talents, energy and time in order merely to save up, protect your future and find satisfaction actually leads to losing yourself to a sad and empty existence. Instead, let us live for the Lord and base our life on love, as Jesus did. In so doing, we will be able to experience genuine joy and our lives will not be empty. They will be fruitful.

SALVATION IS A GIFT THAT
IS GIVEN FREELY

With regard to the love, mercy and divine grace that fill our hearts, there is but one condition: they are free. We cannot buy

3

salvation! Salvation is given freely by the Lord; it is a free gift from God that resides within us. As we have freely received, so are we called upon to give freely (see Matt. 10:8). Let us follow the example of Mary, who, upon receiving the angel's message, immediately shared the gift of her news with her relative, Elizabeth.

Just as everything has been given to us, so it must be shared with others. How? By allowing the Holy Spirit to make us a gift for others. The Spirit is a gift we have received and we, by the power of the Spirit, must be a gift for others, allowing the Holy Spirit to transform us into instruments of acceptance, reconciliation and forgiveness. If our lives are transformed by the grace of the Lord—for the grace of the Lord is indeed transformative—we must not keep the light that shines down from his face only for ourselves, but share it with others so he can illuminate their lives.

A DOCILE HEART

As St. Paul writes, we do not pay for salvation with the blood of bulls and goats (see Heb. 10:4). Since it cannot be bought, for it to reside within, salvation requires our hearts to be humble, docile and obedient.

Thou Virgin Mother, daughter of thy Son,
    Humble and high beyond all other creature,
    The limit fixed of the eternal counsel,

Thou art the one who such nobility
    To human nature gave, that its Creator
    Did not disdain to make himself its creature.

4

Within thy womb rekindled was the love,
   By heat of which in the eternal peace
   After such wise this flower has germinated.

Here unto us thou art a noonday torch
   Of charity, and below there among mortals
   Thou art the living fountain-head of hope.

Lady, thou art so great, and so prevailing,
   That he who wishes grace, nor runs to thee,
   His aspirations without wings would fly.

Not only thy benignity gives succor
   To him who asketh it, but oftentimes
   Forerunneth of its own accord the asking.

In thee compassion is, in thee is pity,
   In thee magnificence; in thee unites
   Whate'er of goodness is in any creature.

Dante Alighieri[1]

HE LOVED US FIRST

His forgiveness and salvation are not things we can buy, or that we acquire through work and efforts. He forgives us and sets us free without cost. His self-sacrifice on the cross is so great that we can never repay him for it; we can only receive it with immense gratitude and with the joy of being more greatly loved than we could ever imagine. "He first loved us" (1 John 4:19).

GOD ALWAYS TAKES THE FIRST STEP TOWARD US

There are two distinct movements: there is the movement of God toward the world, toward humanity—the history of salvation, which culminates in Jesus—and there is the movement of humanity toward God—and here we think of religion, the quest for truth, the journey of nations toward peace, inner peace, justice, freedom. These two movements are driven by a *mutual attraction*. What attracts God to us? Love, for we are his children. He loves us and wants us to be free from evil, sickness, death; he wants to bring us home to his kingdom. God, by his sheer grace, draws us to himself and makes us one with him.

Love and desire come from us, too: goodness attracts us; truth, life, happiness and beauty all attract us.

Jesus is the fulcrum of this mutual attraction, of this dual movement. He is both God and man. But who took the first step? God always does! God's love always comes before our own! He always takes the first step. He waits for us and invites us in; the initiative is always his. Jesus is God made man, he is God incarnate, he was born for us. The new star that appeared in the heavens to the Magi was a sign of the birth of Christ. If those men had not seen the star, they would not have set out.

The light precedes us; truth and beauty precede us. God precedes us. The prophet Jeremiah said that God is like the flower of the almond tree. Why? Because in that part of the world the almond tree is the first to flower (see Jer. 1:11–12). And God is always the first; He is always the first to seek us out and take the first step forward. God always precedes us. His grace precedes us—and this grace appeared in Jesus.

WE WERE SAVED IN THE NAME OF LOVE

Christ sacrificed himself in the name of love to save you. His outstretched arms on the cross are the most telling sign that he is a friend who is willing to stop at nothing: "Having loved his own who were in the world, he loved them to the end" (John 13:1).

THE FIRST STEPS TOWARD TRUE HAPPINESS

Fasting allows us to begin changing our attitude toward others and toward all of creation because it turns us away from the temptation of "devouring" everything and thus satisfying our voracity. Instead, it allows us to prepare to suffer for love, which can fill the emptiness of our hearts.

Through *prayer* we learn to abandon idolatry and egoistic self-sufficiency and instead acknowledge our need for the Lord and his mercy.

Giving alms leads us away from the foolish tendency to accumulate things for ourselves in the illusory belief that they will help us secure a future that is not our own.

Taking these steps, we rediscover the joy of God's plan for creation and for each one of us: to love him, our brothers and sisters and the entire world. Taking these steps, we find true happiness.

HEAVEN CAN'T BE PAID FOR WITH MONEY

When Jesus preaches about life to us, he tells us how we will be judged. He will not say things like, "You can come with me because you made so many important donations to the Church; you are one of its benefactors, so you can come into heaven." No. Entry to heaven is not bought with money. He will not say things like, "You are very important; you have studied many years and received so many honors, so you can come into heaven." No. Not even honors open the doors to heaven.

What, according to Jesus, will open the doors of heaven to us? "I was hungry and you gave me something to eat...I was a stranger and you invited me in...I was ill and you looked after me, I was in prison and you came to visit me" (Matt. 25:35–6). Jesus is humility.

NOT LUXURY, WEALTH OR POWER

Neither luxury, nor great wealth, nor power lead to heaven. Humility is the way. The poor, the ill, the imprisoned and, if they repent, even the greatest sinners will all precede us into heaven. They have the key to open the door to heaven. Those who perform acts of charity will be embraced by the Lord's mercy.

To Hope
O hope! Dear one, busy with kindness!
You who will not scorn the mourner's house,
 Gladly you serve us, noble one,
  Working between mortals and high gods.

Where are you? I've hardly lived, but even now
I feel evening's chill breath steal over me.
   And still, silent as shades, I wait here; and now
     In my breast a tuneless, trembling heart

Sleeps. In the green valley, where the fresh spring
Plunges daily from mountain heights,
   And the lovely autumn crocus blooms
     There, in the stillness, dearest, will I

Look for you, or when deep in the night
Invisible life stirs in the wood,
   And over me the ever-blooming stars
     Like smiling, radiant flowers shine,

O daughter of the Air, come forth then
From your father's gardens, and if you may
   Not come a ghost of the earth, then
     Stir, O stir my heart with wilder fears.

                  Friedrich Hölderlin[2]

WHAT SHOULD WE DO?

Chapter 3 of the Gospel of Luke presents us with various groups of people who, moved by John the Baptist's preaching, ask, "What should we do then?" (Luke 3:10). This question arises from a sense of duty. When the heart is moved by the Lord and when there is enthusiasm for his coming, people are led to ask, "What should we do?"

John replies, "One who is more powerful than I will come" (Luke 3:16). So *what should we do?*

Here is an example: imagine a loved one is coming to visit. We await them joyfully and impatiently. To welcome them properly, we clean the house, prepare the best meal possible, maybe even get them a gift. In other words, we get to work. So it is with the Lord. The joy of his coming forces us to ask, "What should we do?" The thought of God raises this question to a higher level: what should I do with my life? What am I called to? What will complete me?

By suggesting we ask ourselves this question, the Gospel reminds us of something important: life has a task for us. Life is not meaningless; nothing is left to chance. No! Life is a gift the Lord grants us, while also saying: find out who you truly are and work hard to make the dream that is your life come true! Each of us—and let us not forget this—is a mission that needs to be accomplished.

So let us not be afraid to ask the Lord, "What should I do?" Let us ask him this question often. It also recurs in the Bible. In the Acts of the Apostles, upon hearing Peter proclaim Jesus' resurrection, several people "were cut to the heart and said to Peter and the other apostles, 'Brothers, what shall we do?'" (Acts 2:37).

Let us ask ourselves the question: what should I do that would be good for me and for my brothers and sisters? How can I contribute to the well-being of the Church and to the well-being of society?

THE ROAD TO HAPPINESS

Jesus is the Son-made-Servant, sent into the world to save us all through the cross, fulfilling the plan of salvation. His full adherence to God's will renders his *humanity transparent to the glory of God, who is love.*

Listen to Jesus. He is the Savior: follow him. Listening to Christ means taking up the logic of the Easter mystery, setting out on a journey with him to be the gift of love to others, obeying the will of God with docility, taking on an attitude of inner freedom and detaching from worldly things. One must be ready to lose their life, to give it up, so that all people might be saved: in so doing we will meet in eternal happiness (see Mark 8:35).

The path of Jesus always leads to happiness: do not forget this. Always. There may be crosses to bear, there may be trials, but in the end we will always be led to happiness. Jesus does not deceive us; he promised us happiness and he will give it to us if we follow his path.

TRUST IN THE FREEDOM
OF THE GIFT OF GOD

If you do not trust in the freedom of the salvation of the Lord, you will not find salvation.

None of us deserves salvation. None of us! "But I pray, I fast..." you might say. This is good, but without accepting that salvation is given freely, we do not stand a chance. We remain empty, incapable. Everyone. Incapable of following a life of grace, incapable of going to heaven, incapable of conceiving of holiness.

People say, "Father, I am Catholic, I go to Mass on Sunday, I belong to this or that association."

And I reply, "Tell me, do you think you can buy salvation doing that? Do you think all this will save you?"

Your salvation will be helped only if you believe in the freedom of the gift of God. Then all is grace.

KNOWING HOW TO SEE GRACE

My eyes have seen your salvation. We say these words every evening at Compline. With them, we bring our day to an end: "Lord, *my* salvation comes from *you*, my hands are not empty, but are full of your grace." *Knowing how to see grace* is the starting point. We need to look back and reread our life stories and find God's faithful gift, not only in life's grand moments, but also in our fragility and weakness, in our insignificance.

The tempter, the devil, focuses on our "wretchedness," our empty hands. He says things to us like, "After all these years, you still haven't got any better, you still haven't achieved all you could have, they don't let you do what you were cut out to do, you haven't always been faithful, you aren't capable of it..." and so on. Each one of us hears accusations like these. We feel that some of it is true, so we have disorienting thoughts and feelings. We risk losing our way, losing our compass, which is the gratuitous love of God. God always loves us and he gives himself to us, even in our wretchedness.

St. Jerome offered much to the Lord and the Lord kept asking for more. Then St. Jerome said to the Lord, "But Lord, I have given you everything I have, everything. What is missing?"

The Lord replied, "Your sins, give me your sins."[3]

When we keep our gaze fixed on him, we open ourselves to his forgiveness that renews us: we are reassured by his faithfulness.

"Well—very briefly, I should say this: Catholics say that God can be perceived by reason; that from the arrangements of the world they can deduce that there must have been an Arranger—a Mind, you understand. Then they say that they deduce other things about God—that He is Love, for example, because of happiness—"

"And the pain?" she interrupted.

He smiled again.

"Yes. That is the point—that is the weak point."

"But what do they say about that?"

"Well, briefly, they say that pain is the result of sin—"

"And sin? You see, I know nothing at all, Mr. Francis."

"Well, sin is the rebellion of man's will against God's."

"What do they mean by that?"

"Well, you see, they say that God wanted to be loved by His creatures, so He made them free; otherwise they could not really love. But if they were free, it means that they could if they liked refuse to love and obey God; and that is what is called Sin. You see what nonsense—"

She jerked her head a little.

"Yes, yes," she said. "But I really want to get at what they think . . . Well, then, that is all?"

Mr. Francis pursed his lips.

"Scarcely," he said; "that is hardly more than what they call Natural Religion. Catholics believe much more than that."

"Well?"

"My dear Mrs. Brand, it is impossible to put it in a few words. But, in brief, they believe that God became man—that Jesus was God, and that He did this in order to save them from sin by dying—"

"By bearing pain, you mean?"

"Yes; by dying. Well, what they call the Incarnation is really the point. Everything else flows from that."

Robert Hugh Benson[4]

ALL IS FREE, ALL IS GRACE

Evangelical preaching is born freely from the state of awe brought about by salvation; what I have freely received I give freely to others.

"Freely you have received; freely give" (Matt. 10:8): these words contain all the freedom of salvation. We cannot preach or declare the reign of God without this inner certainty that all is gratuitous, all is grace.

The kingdom is like a seed that God gives us. It is a gift that is given freely.

To proclaim the Gospel, we need to have traveled the road of poverty, to have witnessed poverty. "I have no wealth; my wealth is only the riches I have received from God. This gratuitousness is our wealth," we need to say to ourselves. This kind of poverty saves us from being merely administrators and businesspeople. The work of the Church needs to be carried forward, but it needs to be done with a heart that knows poverty.

THE NARROW DOOR

The Gospel of Luke invites us to reflect on the theme of salvation. Jesus was journeying from Galilee toward Jerusalem when someone came up to him and asked, "Lord, are only a few people going to be saved?" (Luke 13:23). Jesus did not answer the question directly; it is not important to know how many people will be saved, but rather which path they need to take that leads to salvation. And so Jesus replied by saying, "Make every effort to enter through the narrow door, because many, I tell you, will try to enter and will not be able to" (verse 24). What does Jesus mean? Which door should we walk through? Why does Jesus define it as being narrow?

The image of the door recurs in the Gospel on several occasions, calling to mind the doors to our homes: places of safety, love and warmth. Jesus tells us that there is a door that gives us access to God's family, to the warmth of God's house and of communion with him. This door is Jesus himself (see John 10:9). He is the door. He is the path to salvation. He leads us to the Father. The door that is Jesus is never closed, it is always open to all, it makes no distinctions and excludes no one; all people are treated equally. Jesus does not exclude anyone.

Some of you may say to me, "But, Father, I am definitely excluded because I am a great sinner: I have done terrible things, I have done so many bad things in my life." No, you are not excluded! It is for this precise reason that you are his favorite; Jesus calls sinners so that he can forgive them, so he can love them. Jesus awaits you so that he can embrace you and forgive you. Do not be afraid: he is waiting for you. Take heart, find the courage to go through his door. Everyone is invited to cross the threshold, the threshold of faith, to enter into his life and to have him enter each of ours so that he may transform it, renew it and give it full and lasting joy.

LIGHT OR SHADOWS

The presence of Jesus in our world forces us to make choices: those who choose darkness will be judged and condemned; those who choose light will be judged and receive salvation. Judgment is the consequence of free choice, which is available to everyone. Those who do evil seek out darkness; evil always hides and covers itself. Those who seek the truth, who do good, come into the light, illuminate the path of life. Those who walk in the light, who approach the light, can only do good works.

This is what we are called upon to do with even greater dedication during Lent: to welcome the light into our consciences and to open our hearts to God's infinite love and his merciful tenderness, goodness and forgiveness. Do not forget that God always forgives—always!—if we humbly ask for forgiveness. It is enough to ask for forgiveness and he will forgive. In so doing, we can find true joy and rejoice in God's forgiveness, which both regenerates and gives life.

RECOLLECTION AND MEMORY

The memory of salvation resides within all of us. But does this memory feel fresh? Or is it a distant, dusty memory, as if it were in a museum? When the memory is not at hand, it gradually transforms into a simple recollection. This is why Moses told his people to go, every year, to the Temple and to show their appreciation by presenting the fruits of the earth, but also, every year, to remember where they came from and how they were saved. When the memory of salvation comes to us, two things happen: our hearts are warmed and we feel joy. A memory that has been subdued, however, moves off and becomes a mere recollection; it neither warms the heart nor gives us joy.

The encounter with memory is an event of salvation, an encounter with the love of God who has made history with us and saved us. The fact that we have been saved is so beautiful that we need to celebrate. When God comes to us, when he approaches us, it is always a cause for celebration. And yet, frequently, we Christians are afraid to celebrate; often, life leads us only to preserve a past memory of salvation and not the awareness that it is alive. Our very Lord told us, "Do this in remembrance of me" (Luke 22:19). But what happens to us is that we distance this memory and transform it into a recollection; it becomes a mere ritual event. We must ask the Lord for the grace to keep his memory at hand, nearby, not subdued into a routine, not a distant recollection.

THE DESERTS OF TODAY

The voice of John the Baptist can still be heard crying out in the deserts of today.

What are today's deserts? They are closed minds and hardened hearts. His voice incites us to ask ourselves if we are actually following the right path, following a life according to the Gospel. Today, as back then, he admonishes us with the words of the prophet Isaiah: "Prepare the way for the LORD" (Isa. 40:3; Matt. 3:3). His words are an urgent request to open our hearts and welcome the salvation that God continuously, almost obstinately, offers us: he wants us to be free from enslavement to sin. But the text of the prophet amplifies this voice and announces that all people will see the salvation of God (Isa. 40:5; Luke 3:6). For salvation is offered to all people—all of us; no one is excluded. None of us can say, "I am a saint, I am perfect; I have already been saved." No. And we must always accept this offer of salvation.

THE ILLUSION OF SAVING OURSELVES

The Lord does not save us with a missive or with a decree; he has already saved us with his love. He became one of us; he walked among us. At Easter, the Lord did two things: he restored people's lost dignity, which is salvation, and he gave us back the dignity we had lost. This, in turn, gives us hope. This dignity will carry us forward until our definitive encounter with him. This is the path of salvation; this is love. We are worthy of it; we are men and women of hope.

Sometimes, however, we want to save ourselves and even believe that we can. We say to ourselves, "I can save myself. I can save myself with money. I am secure, I have money, there will be no problems...I have dignity, the dignity of being rich." But all that is not enough. Think of the parable of the man whose barn is so full of grain he needs to build another one, after which he thinks he can rest easy. But to this the Lord responds, "You fool! This very night your life will be demanded from you" (Luke 12:20). That kind of salvation is wrong. It is temporary, effective in appearance alone and offers the illusion that we can save ourselves through vanity and pride; we believe we are powerful by masking our poverty and sins with vanity and pride.

The truly happy life is one free of all evil, where the highest good will never be lost... This is the reward of the pious; in the hope of attaining it we lead this temporal and mortal life not so much with pleasure as with endurance. And we bear its evils bravely with a good heart and by the gift of God when we rejoice over God's faithful promise of eternal goods and over our faithful expectation of them. The apostle Paul exhorted us to this; he said, *Rejoice in hope; be patient in tribulation.* For he shows why we should be patient in tribulation by prefacing it with the words, Rejoice in hope...

If, then, true virtue delights us, let us say to him what we read in his sacred books, *I shall love you, O Lord, my virtue.* And if we want to be truly happy, something we cannot fail to want, let us hold on to with a believing heart what we learned in the same books: *Happy is the man for whom the name of the Lord is his hope and who has not searched after vanities and insane lies.*

St. Augustine[5]

LET'S ASK OURSELVES WHY WE GOSSIP

Sometimes we get busy doing so many things all at once—and good things, too—but what is really going on within? Who inspires us to do one thing or another? What are our spiritual tendencies? Our daily lives are a bit like a road: when we travel down it, we only look at things that interest us and not at other things.

Our struggle is constantly between grace and sin, between the Lord who wants to save us by pulling us away from temptation and the evil spirit who wants to cast us down in defeat. It is important to recognize what is going on within. It is important to look inward and not let the soul become like a road that everyone can trample.

Before the end of the day, take two or three minutes to ask yourself, "What happened of importance within me today? Oh yes, I was hateful, I spoke badly about people, I did this or that charitable work..." Who influenced you to do these things, whether bad or good? Let us ask ourselves these questions so we can understand what is happening inside. Sometimes, when we indulge the gossipy side of our souls, we learn about everything going on in our neighborhood and everything going on in our neighbor's house, but we do not actually know what is happening within us.

THE REAL FALL IS NOT ACCEPTING HELP

We are saved by Jesus: he loves us; it is in his nature. We can do any number of things against him, but he loves us and saves us. For only what is loved can be saved. Only what is embraced can be transformed. The Lord's love is greater than all our problems, frailties and flaws. But it is precisely with these problems, frailties and flaws that he wants to write our love story. He embraced the prodigal son, he embraced Peter after his denials and he always, always embraces us after every fall, helping us get back on our feet.

The worst fall—and pay attention to this—the worst fall, the one that can ruin our lives, is when we stay down and do not allow ourselves to be helped up.

Mercy and truth
have met together.
Righteousness and bliss
shall kiss one another.
Man, in his foolishness
and shortsightedness,
believes he must make
choices in this life.
He trembles
at the risks he takes.
We all know...
fear.
But no.
Our choice
is of no importance.
The moment comes
when our eyes are opened,
and we see and realize
that grace is infinite.
We need only await it
with confidence
and acknowledge it
in gratitude.
Grace makes no conditions.
And see!
That which we have chosen
is given us...

and that which we have refused . . .
is also granted us.
Yes, that which we rejected
is granted us.
Mercy and truth
have met together.
Righteousness and bliss . . .
shall kiss one another.

Babette's Feast[6]

LET YOURSELF BE RAISED UP BY HIS INFINITE LOVE

The same Christ who saved us from our sins on the cross continues to save and redeem us today by the power of his total self-surrender. Look up at him on the cross, cling to him, let him save you, for those who accept his offer of salvation are set free from sin, sorrow, inner emptiness and loneliness. And if you sin and stray from him, he will come and help you up with the power of his cross. Never forget that he forgives us seventy times seven (see Matt. 18:22). Time and time again, he will carry us on his shoulders. No one can strip us of the dignity bestowed upon us by this boundless and unfailing love. With infinite tenderness, always capable of restoring our joy, he makes it possible for us to lift our heads and start over.

THE JOY OF BEING SAVED

Jesus enters Jerusalem to die on the cross. And it is precisely here that his kingship shines forth in godly fashion: his royal throne is the wood of the cross! Why the cross? Because Jesus takes on the evil, the filth and the sins of the world, including all our sins, and he cleanses them with his blood, with the mercy and love of God. Look around: how many wounds are inflicted upon humanity by evil! Wars, violence, economic conflicts that strike the weak the hardest, greed for money, love of power, corruption, division, crimes against humanity, crimes against creation! And then there are—as each one of us knows—our personal sins: the failure to love and respect God, our neighbor and all of creation.

Jesus on the cross feels the weight of all this evil; with the power of God's love, he is able to conquer it; he defeats it through his resurrection. Jesus helps us all by being on the throne of the cross. If we embrace the cross of Christ with love, we do not experience sadness but joy, the joy of having been saved.

BE HOLY!

One does not need to be a bishop, priest or member of a religious order to be holy. People often think that holiness is only for people who can withdraw from everyday matters and spend a great deal of time in prayer. That is not so. We can all be holy by living our lives with love and by bearing witness in everything we do, wherever we find ourselves.

Do you feel called to the consecrated life? Be holy by living your commitment with joy. Are you married? Be holy by loving and caring for your wife or husband, as Christ does for the Church. Do you work for a living? Be holy by laboring with integrity and skill in the service of your brothers and sisters. Are you a parent or grandparent? Be holy by patiently teaching your little ones how to follow Jesus. Are you in a position of authority? Be holy by working for the common good and renouncing personal gain.

DO NOT BE AFRAID OF HOLINESS

Do not be afraid of holiness. It will take away none of your energy, vitality or joy. On the contrary, you will become the person that the Father had in mind when he created you; you will be faithful to your deepest self. Depending on God sets us free from all forms of enslavement and allows us to recognize our great dignity.

DO NOT BE AFRAID OF SETTING YOUR SIGHTS HIGHER

Do not be afraid to set your sights higher, to allow yourself to be loved and liberated by God. Do not be afraid to let yourself be guided by the Holy Spirit. Holiness does not make you less human; it is an encounter between your frailties and the power of God's grace.

WHEN PUT TO THE TEST, LOOK FORWARD AND NOT TO THE PAST

Peter writes, "Be holy in all you do; for it is written: 'Be holy, because I am holy'" (1 Pet. 1:15–16).

Even if it is not easy to be as holy as our heavenly Father, the model for being holy is simple. Too often we think of holiness as if it were something extraordinary, as if it means having visions or saying only the loftiest prayers. Many people think that being holy means having the face of a saint, looking like a saint. But being holy is something else entirely: it means walking toward holiness, walking toward the light or grace that comes toward you. It's odd how when we walk toward a bright light we are often blinded and cannot see the road in front of us, and yet we do not make any mistakes; by following the light, we follow the road.

Walking toward the light means walking toward holiness. Even if we cannot see the road well, the light guides us toward hope. And walking toward holiness brings us closer to the encounter with Jesus Christ.

To walk in this manner, we must be free and feel free, but many things enslave us. To this end, Peter gives us some advice: "As obedient children, do not conform to the evil desires you had when you lived in ignorance" (1 Pet. 1:14). Do not conform, do not go back to the old patterns of the world, those mundane ways of thinking and judging that the world offers you. They will strip you of your freedom.

To approach holiness you need to be free: free to walk and look at the light, free to move toward it. When we go back to the ways of life we had before our encounter with Jesus Christ, when we return to our old patterns of the world, we lose our freedom.

In moments of difficulty, we are tempted to return to our old ways, to accept the patterns of the world that caused us to lose freedom. But without freedom we cannot be holy: we need to be free in order to see and walk toward the light.

What will you do when you are put to the test? Will you continue looking forward, or will you give up your freedom and hide in the mundane patterns of the world, which promise everything but give nothing?

Let us ask for the grace to understand how to walk in holiness, how to follow the path of freedom that fills us with hope and leads us toward the encounter with Jesus.

DO NOT BECOME SLAVES OF FALSE FREEDOMS

The word "redemption" is not often used but it is fundamental because it indicates the most radical liberation God could possibly provide for us, for all of humanity, for all of creation.

It would seem that people today no longer want to think they have been freed and saved by God's intervention; people exist under the illusion that they can attain everything through freedom. They boast about it. But, actually, this is not the case. How many illusions are sold on the pretext of freedom; how many new forms of slavery have been created under the guise of false freedom!

So many people are enslaved. "I do it because I want to; I take drugs because I like them; I'm free to do it if I want; I like doing it," they say. But really they are slaves! They become slaves in the name of freedom. We all know people like this—and their lives end up ruined. We need God to free us from all forms of indifference, selfishness and illusions of self-sufficiency.

SHARING IS TRUE HAPPINESS

God does not reveal himself to us cloaked in worldly power and wealth, but rather in weakness and poverty. "Though he was rich, yet for your sake he became poor" (2 Cor. 8:9). Christ, the eternal Son of God, One with the Father in power and glory, chose to become poor; he came among us and drew near to each of us; he set aside his glory and emptied himself so that he could be like us in all things (see Phil. 2:7; Heb. 4:15). The incarnation of God is a great mystery! But the reason behind it all is his divine love. His love is grace, generosity and the desire to be near us; he does not hesitate to offer himself in sacrifice for us, his beloved. Charity and love mean sharing in the destiny of the loved one. Love unites us, it creates equality, it breaks down walls and eliminates distances. God has done all of this with us.

Jesus' goal in making himself poor was not to seek poverty for its own sake but, as St. Paul says, "so that you through his poverty might become rich" (2 Cor. 8:9). This is not a mere play on words or a catchphrase. On the contrary, it summarizes God's logic, the logic of love, the logic of the incarnation and the cross. God did not drop salvation down from heaven like a person who has extra money to spend might give to a charity with a kind of philanthropic piety. Christ's love is entirely different! When Jesus stepped into the waters of the Jordan and was baptized by John the Baptist, he did not do it to repent or convert; he did it to be among people who are needy for forgiveness, to be among us sinners, to take upon himself the burden of our sins. This is the path he chose to console us, to save us and to free us from our misery. It is notable how the apostle points out that we were set free not by Christ's riches, but by *his poverty.*

So how can we describe the poverty that Christ takes on, which frees and enriches us? It is his way of loving us, his way of assisting us, just like the Good Samaritan assisted the half-dead man who had been left by the side of the road. What give us true freedom, true salvation and true happiness are the compassion, tenderness and solidarity of his love. The poverty of Christ that enriches us is his incarnation, the way he takes on our weaknesses and sins. It is an expression of God's infinite mercy.

LET US LEARN TO WELCOME OUR WEAKNESSES

The history of salvation is accomplished "against all hope" (Rom. 4:18), which is to say through our weaknesses. All too often, we think that God only relies on the parts of us that are good, when actually most of his plans come to fruition thanks to, and because of, our weaknesses. This is what led St. Paul to say:

> In order to keep me from becoming conceited, I was given a thorn in my flesh, a messenger of Satan, to torment me. Three times I pleaded with the Lord to take it away from me. But he said to me, "My grace is sufficient for you, for my power is made perfect in weakness."
>
> (2 Cor. 12:7–9)

IF THE FOUNDATION OF SALVATION RESTS ON THIS, WE MUST LEARN TO LOOK UPON OUR WEAKNESSES WITH PROFOUND TENDERNESS

The evil one would have us see and condemn our weaknesses while the Spirit holds them tenderly in the light. This is the best way to handle our weaknesses: with tenderness. Pointing fingers and judging others are frequently signs of an inability to accept our own weaknesses and shortcomings. Only tender love will save us from the accuser. This is why it is so important to encounter God's mercy, especially in the sacrament of reconciliation, where we experience his truth and tenderness. Paradoxically, the evil one can also speak the truth but does so only in order to condemn us. We know that God's truth does not condemn but instead welcomes, embraces, sustains and forgives us.

THE GRACE OF GOD TRANSFORMS OUR HEARTS

How inscrutable are the ways of the Lord! We experience this every day, and especially when we think back to the times the Lord called to us. Let us never forget the time and the way that God first entered our lives. Let us always retain the memory of that encounter with grace, when God transformed our lives and became part of our hearts and minds.

How often, in the face of the Lord's great works, does the question arise: how is it possible that God uses a sinner, a frail and weak person, to do his will? And yet, nothing happens by chance; everything is part of God's plan. He weaves each of our stories, each of our life histories. He weaves our stories and, if we trust in his plan for salvation, we understand this. The calling always implies a mission to which we are destined; for this reason we are asked to prepare ourselves with seriousness. God himself calls to us; God himself sustains us with his grace. Brothers and sisters, let us be guided by the following awareness: grace, in its supremacy, transforms existence and makes us worthy of being placed at the service of the

Gospel. Supreme grace covers all sins, changes hearts, changes lives and makes us see new paths. Let us not forget this.

LOVE IS ALWAYS FREEDOM

Salvation takes place because of Jesus. However, salvation is not automatic; salvation is a gift of love and, as such, it is offered to humans who then experience freedom. Whenever we speak of love, we speak of freedom. Love without freedom is not love; it may be interest or fear but not love. Love is always free and, being free, it calls for a response that is given freely: it calls for our *conversion*. In other words, it means changing our way of thinking—this is conversion, changing our way of thinking—and changing our lives: no longer following the examples of the mundane world but those of God.

FORGIVENESS, LOVE AND JOY

By making himself one of us, the Lord Jesus not only takes on the human condition, but also raises us up so that we become children of God. By his death and resurrection, Jesus Christ, the blameless Lamb, conquered death and sin to free us from their dominion. He is the Lamb that was sacrificed for us so that we can receive a new life made up of forgiveness, love and joy.

How beautiful these three words are: forgiveness, love and joy. All that he took on was redeemed, freed and saved. Even so, life puts us to the test. We often suffer. In these moments, we are invited to turn our gaze to the crucified Jesus who suffers for us and with us as proof that God does not abandon us. Let us never forget that when we feel anguish and persecution, as well as everyday sufferings, we are liberated by the merciful hand of God who raises us up to him and leads us to a new life.

REDEEM YOURSELF AND BE SAVED BY LOVE

God's love is boundless: we continuously discover new signs that reveal his care for us and, above all, his wish to reach and precede us. Our entire lives, while marked by the fragility of sin, are visible to God who loves us. How many pages of sacred Scripture speak to us of God's presence, his closeness and tenderness for all people, and especially the young, the poor and the troubled! God has great tenderness and love for the youngest among us, for the weakest, for those cast out by society. The greater our need, the more his gaze upon us is filled with mercy. He feels compassion and pity for us because he knows our weaknesses. He knows our sins and forgives us. He always forgives! Our Father is so very good.

Let us therefore open up to the Lord and receive his grace! Because, as Psalm 130:7 says, "For with the LORD is unfailing love and with him is full redemption."

PEARLS ARE BORN FROM OUR WOUNDS

Mary was little more than an adolescent and yet, in the Magnificat (Luke 1:46–55), she echoed the praises of her people and their history. This shows us how being young does not necessarily mean being disconnected from the past. Our personal history is part of a long trail, a communal journey that has preceded us over the ages. Like Mary, we belong to a people. History teaches us that, even when the Church has to sail on stormy seas, the hand of God guides her and helps her overcome moments of difficulty. The Church is not like a flash mob, where people agree to meet, put on a performance and then go their separate ways. The Church is heir to a long tradition that has been passed down from generation to generation and is further enriched by the experience of each individual. Your personal history has a place within the greater history of the Church.

Being mindful of the past helps us be open to the unexpected ways that God acts in us and through us. It helps us stay open to the possibility that we could be chosen to be his instruments and help him bring about salvation.

How do you "save" in your memory the events and experiences of your life? What do you do with the facts and the images that are part of your memory? Some people, those who have been particularly hurt by certain situations in life, may want to "erase" their pasts; they claim the right to forget it all. But I would like to remind you that there is no saint without a past and no sinner without a future. Pearls are born in the wound of an oyster! Jesus, with his love, can heal our hearts and turn our lives into genuine pearls.

EVERY INSTANT IN LIFE IS PRECIOUS

Jesus invites us to recognize within ourselves the need for God and his grace, to have a balanced attitude with regard to material goods, to be welcoming and humble toward all, to know ourselves and to find fulfillment in the encounter with others and by doing service for them. The amount of time available to each of us during which we may receive redemption is brief: the duration of our life on earth. It is short. And while life is a gift of God's infinite love, it is also a time for proving our love for him. This is why every moment, every instant of our existence, is precious time for loving God and our neighbors, thereby entering into eternal life.

Our lives follow two rhythms: one is measurable, made up of hours, days and years; the other is composed of the seasons of our development: birth, childhood, adolescence, maturity, old age, death. Both rhythms have their own value; each stage can be a privileged moment of encounter with the Lord. Faith helps us discover the spiritual significance of these periods: each one of them contains a particular calling by the Lord to which we can give either a positive or a negative response. In the Gospel we see how Simon, Andrew, James and John responded to the call: they were mature men, they worked as fishermen, they had their family lives...Yet, when Jesus passed by and called to them, "At once they left their nets and followed him" (Mark 1:18).

Let us be aware and not let Jesus pass by without welcoming him. St. Augustine said that he was afraid of God when he passes by. Why? What was he afraid of? He was afraid of not recognizing him, not seeing him, not welcoming him.

To Recover
If to recover what was recovered
I had to first lose what was lost,
If to obtain the obtainable

I had to bear what was borne,
If to be in love now

33

It was necessary to have been hurt,
I have well suffered what was suffered,
I have well cried what was cried.

Because after everything I have proved
That one cannot enjoy the enjoyable
Until after having suffered.

Because after everything I have understood
That what the tree has visibly in bloom
Thrives of what is buried beneath.

Francisco Luis Bernárdez[7]

THE MOST BEAUTIFUL FLOWERS GROW AMID THE DRIEST ROCKS

Even if we are sinners, and we all are, even if our best intentions exist only on paper or if, when we examine our lives, we realize that we have accumulated many failures, on Easter morning we can be like those people described in the Gospel who go to the sepulcher of Christ, see the large overturned stone and reflect on how God is preparing an unexpected future for each of us. We can visualize God rising from the sepulcher; this place is happiness, joy, life. It is not, as everyone thought, a place of sadness, defeat and shadows. God has his most beautiful flowers grow amid the driest rocks.

PART 2

HAPPINESS IS A GIFT
TO BE GIVEN

UPWARD, TOWARD A
NOBLE DESTINATION

Friends, you were not made merely to get by, to spend your days balancing out your obligations with your pleasures. You were made to soar upward, toward the most genuine, true and beautiful desires that you cherish in your hearts: to love God and serve your neighbors. Do not think that life's great dreams are unattainable and exist only in the clouds. You were made to take flight, to embrace the courage of truth and the beauty of justice, to build a strong moral character, be heart-centered, show compassion, serve others and build relationships, like the Inuuqatigiit principles say.[1] You were made to sow the seeds of peace and loving care wherever you are, to ignite the enthusiasm of those who surround you, to keep pressing forward and not flatten everything out.

But, you might say, living like that is harder than flying! Of course it is not easy: a hidden force of spiritual gravity tries to drag us down, paralyze our desires and weaken our joy. But think of the Arctic tern, which in Spanish we call a *charrán*. It does not let headwinds or sudden changes in temperature stop it from flying from one end of the earth to the other. Sometimes it has to choose alternative routes or take detours; it is forced to adapt to certain winds... but it always sticks to the goal and always reaches its destination.

You will meet people who will try to nullify your dreams, who will tell you to settle for less, to fight only for what is in your interest. When this happens, you will ask yourself: why should I work for what other people do not believe in? Or else: how can I take flight in a world that is constantly troubled by scandals, wars, fraud, injustice, environmental destruction, indifference toward those in need and disillusionment from those who should be setting an example? Faced with such questions, what could the answer possibly be?

You are the answer. You, my brothers and sisters.

If you do not try, you will already have lost. The future is in your hands. The community that gave birth to you, the environment in which you live, the hopes of your peers are all in your hands. Without even asking you, people expect you to bring your singular treasure—your personality—to bear on history. Because each of us truly is unique.

The world you are living in is the treasure you have inherited: love it in the same way that you are loved by the One who gave you life, with all its joys, the way God loves you. He created this beauty for you, he never ceases to have confidence in you, not for a second. He believes in your talents. Each time you seek him out, you will realize how the path he calls you to follow leads upward. You will realize this when you look up at the sky as you pray and especially when you contemplate him on the cross. You will come to realize that Jesus never points his finger down at you from the cross, but embraces and encourages you. He believes in you even when you stop believing in yourself. So never lose hope, fight the good fight, give it your all and you will not be sorry. Go forward on your journey, step by step, toward the best there is.

Set the navigator of your existence on a great destination: upward!

> It's not hard to die well. It's hard to live well.
> *Rome, Open City*[2]

BECOME AN INSTRUMENT OF MERCY

The desire to be close to Christ requires us to draw near to our brothers and sisters. Nothing is more pleasing to the Father than a true sign of mercy. By its very nature, mercy becomes visible and tangible in specific and powerful acts. Once mercy has been truly experienced, it is impossible to turn back: it constantly grows and changes our lives. It's an authentic new creation made by a young heart, one that is capable of loving fully, and it cleanses our eyes so that we can perceive hidden needs. How true are the words of the Church's prayer at the Easter Vigil, after the reading of the story of creation, "O God, who wonderfully created human nature and still more wonderfully redeemed it."[3]

Mercy *renews and redeems* because it is the encounter between two hearts: the heart of God as it approaches the human heart. The latter is warmed and healed by the former. Hearts of stone become hearts of flesh, capable of loving despite our sins. We come to realize that we are a "new creation" (2 Cor. 5:17). I am loved, therefore I exist. I am forgiven, therefore I am reborn. I have been shown mercy, therefore I have become an instrument of mercy.

SOWING PEACE

"Blessed are the peacemakers, for they will be called children of God" (Matt. 5:9). Let us look into the faces of those who go around sowing discord—are they happy? The people who are constantly looking for occasions to mislead and take advantage of others—are they happy? No, they cannot possibly be happy. Meanwhile, those who patiently try to sow the seeds of peace each day, the artisans of peace and reconciliation—they are blessed, they are true children of our heavenly Father, who always and only sows the seeds of peace, to the extent that he even sent his Son into the world as the seed of peace for humanity.

Each of you keep watch over your heart and confess your sins to yourself unceasingly. Be not afraid of your sins, even when perceiving them, if only there be penitence, but make no conditions with God. Again I say, Be not proud. Be proud neither to the little nor to the great. Hate not those who reject you, who insult you, who abuse and slander you. Hate not the atheists, the teachers of evil, the materialists—and I mean not only the good ones— for there are many good ones among them, especially in our day—hate not even the wicked ones. Remember them in your prayers thus: Save, O Lord, all those who have none to pray for them, save too all those who will not pray. And add: it is not in pride that I make this prayer, O Lord, for I am lower than all men...Love God's people, let not strangers draw away the flock, for if you slumber in your slothfulness and disdainful pride, or worse still, in covetousness, they will come from all sides and draw away your flock. Expound the Gospel to the people unceasingly...be not extortionate...Do not love gold and silver, do not hoard them...Have faith. Cling to the banner and raise it on high.

Fyodor Dostoevsky[4]

THE STRENGTH TO CHANGE THINGS

In my years as a bishop, I learned one thing in particular: nothing is more beautiful than seeing the enthusiasm, dedication, zeal and energy with which so many young people live their lives. Where does this beauty come from? When a young person's heart is touched by Jesus, he or she becomes capable of truly great things. It is exciting to listen to a young person share their dreams, ask their questions and show their eagerness to oppose people who say that things simply cannot be changed. I call those people, the ones who say that things simply cannot be changed, "quietists."

NURTURE GREAT IDEALS

Know that Jesus loves you: he is a sincere and faithful friend and will never abandon you; you can trust in him! In moments of doubt—we have all had dark moments when we were young, moments of great doubt—in these times of difficulty, you can count on receiving help from Jesus, who will, above all, nurture your greatest ideals.

I have often heard young people say, "I trust in God, but not in the Church."

Why is that?

"Because I am skeptical of priests."

Ah, you're skeptical of priests? Then go up to a priest and say, "I don't trust you because of this, that and the other." Go up to him! Go up to a bishop and say it to his face! "I don't trust the Church because of this, that and the other." This is what it means to have youthful courage! Maybe the priest will take it badly and wave you away, but that will only happen once. He will reply. But you have to be willing to listen to what he says. Listen!

WE WILL BE JUDGED ON LOVE

We cannot escape the Lord's words. They will be the basis on which we will be judged. We need to feed the hungry and give drink to the thirsty, welcome strangers and clothe the naked, spend time with the sick and those in prison (see Matt. 25:31–45). We will also be asked if we have helped others resolve the doubts that caused them to fall into despair and which are often the source of loneliness; if we have helped educate the millions of people who live without proper schools, especially children deprived of the necessary means to free themselves from the bonds of poverty; if we have been kind to the lonely and afflicted; if we have forgiven those who have offended us and rejected all forms of anger and hatred that lead to violence; if we have shown the same kind of patience to others as God in his great patience has shown us; and, finally, if we have prayed to the Lord for our brothers and sisters.

Christ himself is present in the youngest ones among us. His flesh is visible in the flesh of the tortured, the defeated, the scourged, the malnourished, the exiled... all of whom are waiting to be acknowledged, touched and cared for by us. Let us not forget the words of St. John of the Cross: "In the evening of life, we will be judged on love alone."[5]

WHAT IS YOUR IDENTITY?

Sin, and above all the sin of worldliness, which is as present as the air we breathe, gives rise to a mentality that tends toward the affirmation of oneself against others and against God. When thinking with a worldly mentality, it is difficult for a person to express their identity in positive terms or in terms of salvation; they are more likely to express themselves in negative terms, by saying what they are against. The thought process behind sin does not hesitate to use deceit and violence. And we see what happens: greed, desire for power and not service, war, the exploitation of people.

LET US STEP OUTSIDE OUR COMFORT ZONES

Let us not think of the poor simply as beneficiaries of our occasional volunteer work or our impromptu acts of generosity that appease our conscience. However good and useful such acts may be for making us sensitive to people's needs and the injustices that exist, they ought to lead to a true *encounter* with the poor and a *sharing* that becomes a way of life. Our prayers and our journey of discipleship and conversion find the confirmation of their evangelical authenticity in precisely such charity and sharing. This way of life gives rise to joy and serenity; it helps us come into contact with the *flesh of Christ*.

If we truly wish to encounter Christ, we have to come into contact with the suffering bodies of the poor, as a response to the sacramental communion bestowed in the Eucharist. The body of Christ, which is symbolically broken during the sacred liturgy, can be seen in the faces of our most vulnerable brothers and sisters when we perform acts of charity and sharing. St. John Chrysostom's words are always timely: "If you want to honor the body of Christ, do not scorn it when it is naked; do not honor the Eucharistic Christ with silk vestments, and then, leaving the church, neglect the other Christ suffering from cold and nakedness."[6]

We are called on to reach out to the poor, to go forth and meet them, to look into their eyes and embrace them so they can feel the warmth of love and so we can break through their loneliness. Their outstretched hands are an invitation to leave behind our certainties, to step outside our comfort zones and to acknowledge the value of poverty, in and of itself.

MERCY KNOWS NO LIMITS

To this day, entire populations suffer from hunger and thirst. We are continuously haunted by pictures of children with nothing to eat. Masses of people continue to migrate from one country to another in search of food, work, shelter and peace. Disease, in all its forms, is a constant cause of suffering that requires assistance, comfort and support. Many people confined in prisons also experience serious hardships owing to inhumane living conditions. Illiteracy remains widespread, preventing children from developing their potential and thereby exposing them to new forms of slavery. The culture of extreme individualism, especially in the West, has led to a loss of solidarity with—and responsibility for—others. God himself is unknown to many: this represents the greatest paucity and the largest obstacle to recognizing the inviolable dignity of human life.

Merciful works, both spiritual and physical, continue to this day to be effective proof of the immense positive influence of mercy as a *social value*. Mercy compels us to roll up our sleeves and work to restore dignity to millions of people, our brothers and sisters, who have been called on to build a reliable city with us.

Let us make every effort to enact concrete forms of charity and devise insightful ways of practicing merciful works. By its nature, mercy is inclusive. It spreads like oil on water. It knows no limits. Let us find new ways of expressing the more traditional works of mercy. For mercy always overflows, it always goes beyond, it continuously bears fruit. It is like yeast that makes dough rise (see Matt. 13:33), or the mustard seed that grows into a tree (see Luke 13:19).

OVERCOMING THE TEMPTATION OF INDIFFERENCE

We all need to experience a conversion in how we perceive the poor. We have to care for them and be sensitive to their spiritual and material needs. Faced with old and new forms of poverty—unemployment, migration and addictions of many kinds—we have a duty to be alert and thoughtful; we must overcome the temptation to remain indifferent.

Let us think of those who feel unloved, who have no hope for the future and who have given up on life out of discouragement, disappointment or fear. Speaking with elegant rhetoric about the poor is not enough! Let us spend time with them. Let us go forth and meet them, look into their eyes and listen to them. The poor provide us with a concrete opportunity to encounter Christ and to touch his wounded flesh.

BEING CHRISTIAN MEANS TAKING ACTION

The dignity of people can be attacked in many ways: through unemployment; by not receiving a sufficient salary; by not being able to have a home or land on which to live; by experiencing discrimination on account of one's faith, race or social status. Christian mercy responds to such attacks with vigilance and solidarity.

There are many ways we can restore dignity to people and make their lives better! Think only of the many children who suffer forms of violence that rob them of the joys of life. I see their sorrowful and bewildered faces before me; they are begging for our help to be set free from the bonds of the contemporary world. These children are the young adults of tomorrow. How are we preparing them to live with dignity and responsibility? How can they face their present and their future with hope?

The *social nature* of mercy demands that we do not just stand by, doing nothing. It requires us to end indifference and hypocrisy, so that our plans and projects do not remain words on a page but so they can come to life.

THE PLEASURE OF BEING
A BUBBLING SPRING

Whenever we encounter another person in the name of love, we learn something new about God. Whenever we open our eyes and truly see the other, the light that illuminates our faith grows. With it grows our capacity to recognize God. It follows that, if we want our spiritual life to advance, we must embrace missionary work.

Evangelism enriches the mind and the heart, it opens up spiritual horizons, it makes us more sensitive to the workings of the Holy Spirit and it takes us beyond our limited spiritual constructs. Missionaries who are committed to their work are like bubbling springs, overflowing and refreshing others. This openness of the heart is a source of joy because, "It is more blessed to give than to receive" (Acts 20:35). We do not live better when we flee, hide, refuse to share, stop giving and lock ourselves up in our own comfortable worlds. Such a life is equivalent to a slow suicide.

I AM A MISSION

My mission of being in people's hearts is not just a part of my life, an ornament I can remove, a postscript, or one of the many phases in my life. It is something I cannot extract from my being without destroying my very self. *I am a mission* on this earth; it is the reason I exist in this world.

Essentially, we need to see ourselves as being branded by the mission of bringing light, blessing, enlivening, raising up, healing and freeing. There are nurses with souls, teachers with souls, politicians with souls—people who have made a committed choice to exist with and for others. And yet, the minute a person separates their duties from their personal life, everything goes gray: they seek recognition for their work or assert their needs. That person will become an individual and, consequently, not part of our people.

"The world is all grown strange. Elf and Dwarf in company walk in our daily fields; and folk speak with the Lady of the Wood and yet live; and the Sword comes back to war that was broken in the long ages ere the fathers of our fathers rode into the Mark! How shall a man judge what to do in such times?"

"As he ever has judged," said Aragorn. "Good and ill have not changed since yesteryear; nor are they one thing among Elves and Dwarves and another among Men. It is a man's part to discern them, as much in the Golden Wood as in his own house."

J. R. R. Tolkien[7]

EVERY PERSON IS WORTHY

If we are to share our lives with others and generously give of ourselves, we also have to acknowledge that all people deserve our time and dedication. People should not be evaluated on their physical appearance, their abilities, their language, their way of thinking, or for the satisfaction that might come to us from helping them, but simply because they are God's handiwork, his creation.

God created them in his image; they all reflect something of God's glory. Every human being is the object of God's infinite tenderness. He resides in their lives. Jesus offered his precious blood on the cross for that person.

Appearances notwithstanding, all people are holy and deserve our love. If I can help at least one person lead a better life, then the gift that is my life has been justified. It is a wonderful thing to be God's faithful people. We achieve fulfillment when we break down walls and our heart is filled with faces and names!

NOT WITH WORDS BUT DEEDS

"Dear children, let us not love with words or speech but with actions and in truth" (1 John 3:18). The words of the apostle John articulate an imperative that no Christian should ignore. The seriousness with which the Beloved hands down Jesus' command to our own day is made even clearer by the contrast between the *empty words* so frequently on our lips and the *concrete actions* against which we are called to measure ourselves. Love has no alibi. Whenever we set out to love as Jesus loved, we have to take the Lord as our example, especially when it comes to loving the poor.

The Son of God's way of loving is well known, and John spells it out clearly. It stands on two pillars: God loved us first (see 1 John 4:10, 19), and he loved us by giving himself completely, even laying down his life (see 1 John 3:16).

Such love cannot go unanswered. Even though it is offered unconditionally, asking nothing in return, it sets hearts on fire to such a degree that all who experience it are led to love back, despite their limitations and sins. But this can only happen if we welcome God's grace, which is to say his merciful charity, as fully as possible into our hearts so that our will, and even our emotions, are drawn to love both God and our neighbor. In this way, the mercy that wells up, as it were, from the heart of the Trinity can shape our lives and bring forth compassion and works of mercy for the benefit of our brothers and sisters in need.

BEAR WITNESS WITH YOUR LIFE

All Christians who are baptized in water and the Holy Spirit are called to live as if immersed in an everlasting Easter, and therefore to live as a person who has risen. Do not live like a dead person! Live like one who has risen! This gift is not for us alone; it is meant to be shared with all. The mission can only come into being by sharing this happiness with others.

A beautiful and enriching experience of faith, capable of dealing with life's inevitable hardships, is naturally convincing. When a person speaks about the Gospel through an experience in his or her own life, it breaks through even the hardest of hearts. For this reason, I entrust you to take the key action of the Christian mission: bear witness with your life. As for those who do not bear witness with their own lives, who merely pretend, well, they are like people who hold checks in their hand but don't sign them. Bearing witness means sharing your riches, qualities and vocation. Add your signature! Always!

A TRUE CULTURAL REVOLUTION

We are called on to promote a *culture of mercy* based on encounter with others: a culture where no one looks at another with indifference or turns away from brothers and sisters who suffer. Works of mercy are "handmade" in that no two of them are alike. Our hands can craft them in a thousand different ways even though the God who inspires them is One. Even though they are all fashioned from the same "material," mercy itself, each work takes on a different form.

Works of mercy affect a person's entire life. We can set in motion a true cultural revolution beginning with simple gestures that touch people's lives, bodies and spirits. The Christian community can take ownership of this commitment through the awareness that God constantly asks us to deny the temptation of hiding behind indifference and individualism just so we can lead comfortable lives, free of problems. Jesus says to his disciples, "You will always have the poor among you" (John 12:8). No alibi exists to justify not engaging with the poor after Jesus has identified with each and every one of them.

LIVING TO SERVE

Our credibility as Christians is based on how we welcome outcasts who suffer physically and on how we welcome sinners who suffer spiritually. Not in theory, but in practice!

Humanity today needs men and women who do not want to live their lives "halfway." Humanity needs people who are ready to give their lives freely in service to their brothers and sisters who are poor and vulnerable, just as Christ gave himself for our salvation. When faced with evil, suffering and sin, the only possible response for a disciple of Jesus is to give oneself, even one's own life, in imitation of Christ. This is what it means to serve. If Christians do not live to serve, their lives do not serve a greater purpose. Jesus gave up his life to serve.

TAKE CARE OF YOUR BROTHERS AND SISTERS

Taking care means living charity in a dynamic and intelligent way. Today we need people, especially young people, who have eyes that can see to the needs of the weakest, people with large hearts so they can give of themselves entirely.

You are called upon to use your skills and place your intelligence at the service of a wide range of charitable projects. Today it is your turn, but you are not the first! How many Good Samaritans have lived out their missions by caring for wounded brothers and sisters they encountered along the way! Follow in their footsteps, but in a style and manner suited to our times. It is your turn to carry out effective and well-planned charitable acts, to show charity with imagination and intelligence, not periodically but regularly, over a long period of time, helping people on their journey of healing and growth.

This is the verb that I entrust to you: *take care* of your brothers and sisters. Do it without selfishness, in the name of service and in order to help.

People worked and struggled, each set in motion by the mechanism of his own cares. But the mechanisms would not have worked properly had they not been regulated and governed by a higher sense of an ultimate freedom from care. This freedom came from the feeling that all human lives were interrelated, a certainty that they flowed into each other—a happy feeling that all events took place not only on the earth, in which the dead are buried, but also in some other region which some called the Kingdom of God.

Boris Pasternak[8]

"FREELY YOU HAVE RECEIVED; FREELY GIVE"

The lives of people who do not give freely of themselves become frenetic and commercial; they are too busy measuring out what they give and what they receive. God gives freely, to the extent that he even helps those who are unfaithful: "He causes his sun to rise on the evil and the good" (Matt. 5:45). This is why Jesus told us, "But when you give to the needy, do not let your left hand know what your right hand is doing, so that your giving may be in secret" (Matt. 6:3–4).

We received life freely; we paid nothing for it. We should give without expecting anything in return. Do good things for others without expecting them to return the favor. As Jesus told his disciples, "Freely you have received; freely give" (Matt. 10:8).

SOLIDARITY, COOPERATION, RESPONSIBILITY

Solidarity, cooperation and responsibility represent three pillars of the Church's social teaching, which sees people who are open to building relationships as the summit of creation and the center of the social, economic and political order. Based on this vision—while being sensitive to humankind and historical processes—the Church's social doctrine contributes to a vision of the world that is opposed to individualism: it has the common good of all people as its goal.

At the same time, the Church's social doctrine is opposed to a collectivistic vision that is currently re-emerging in a new form and which lies hidden behind projects of technocratic standardization. Solidarity, cooperation and responsibility: three words that recall the mystery of God himself, the Trinity. God, as the unification of humanity, inspires us to find fulfillment in being generous and open to others (solidarity), through collaboration with others (cooperation) and through commitment to others (responsibility). We are inspired to do all this at every level of society, in our personal relationships, in our professional and civic duties, in our relationship with creation and in the way we participate in political life.

In every sphere of life, now more than ever, we need to show concern for others, step out of our own worlds and commit freely to the development of a more just and equitable society, a society where selfishness and partisan interests do not prevail. At the same time, we are called on to be vigilant in upholding respect for all people and their freedoms, thereby safeguarding their inviolable dignity. This is the mission; this is how we should implement the Church's social doctrine.

BLESSED ARE OPEN HANDS

We know how hard it is, in our contemporary world, to see poverty for what it clearly is. And yet we are challenged by it in myriad ways every single day. We see it in faces marked by suffering, marginalization, oppression, violence, torture and imprisonment, war, the deprivation of freedom and dignity, ignorance and illiteracy, medical emergencies, lack of work, trafficking and slavery, exile, extreme destitution and forced migration. We see poverty on the faces of women, men and children exploited by base interests and crushed by the ruses that lie behind power and money. When we think of the forms of destitution that are the results of social injustice, moral degeneration, generalized indifference and greed, what a cruel and endless list it is!

Tragically, in this day and age, while the privileged few continue to accumulate ostentatious wealth, often in conjunction with illegal activities and the exploitation of human dignity, poverty is extending in scandalous ways around the world and through broad sectors of society. Faced with this scenario, we cannot remain passive, much less resigned. Think of the poverty that stifles the spirit of initiative of so many young people, keeping them from finding work. Think of the poverty that dulls the sense of personal responsibility, leaving others to do the work while some go looking for preferential treatment. Think of the poverty that poisons the pool of possible candidates for employment, limiting all notions of professionalism and humiliating those who deserve to work and be productive. We must respond to all these forms of poverty with a new vision of life and society.

Blessed, therefore, are the open hands that embrace the poor and offer help: they are hands that bring hope. Blessed are the hands that reach beyond all barriers of culture, religion and nationality, offering the balm of consolation to the wounds of humanity. Blessed are the hands that open without asking for anything in exchange. These are the hands that bring God's blessing to our brothers and sisters.

GET YOUR HANDS DIRTY
AND YOU WILL BE HAPPY

A competitive person's hands take continuously but also remain closed. They take by accumulating, often at a high price and always at the expense of nullifying or hoping to depreciate others. Instead, the gesture related to anti-competition is one of opening. Opening up, being in movement. Competition generally happens at a standstill: it does its math, often unconsciously, but is always still; it does not make itself available. A person matures, however, while in movement, while walking, when they make themselves available.

To say it in simple words, a person matures if they get their hands dirty. Why? Because their hand is outreached and open, ready to wave, embrace, receive. "It is more blessed to give than to receive" (Acts 20:35). The mindset of accumulation, which leaves no room for emotion, is countered by the act of doing service.

Young people who are mature—those who are confident, smiling, with a sense of humor—have open hands. They have set out and are on a journey. They are the ones who take risks. If you never take risks, you will never mature, you will never be able to prophesy, you will only have the illusion of accumulating in the name of security. I think of the parable about the rich man who had so much grain that he did not know where to store it. "I will tear down my barns and build bigger ones, and there I will store my surplus grain...Take life easy: eat, drink and be merry" (Luke 12:18–19). He protected himself. But Jesus says that the story ended with God saying, "You fool! This very night your life will be demanded from you. Then who will get what you have prepared for yourself?" (Luke 12:20).

The culture of competition never talks about the end of life, only the ends we want to achieve in life through accumulating, climbing and reaching in every way possible, always crushing people beneath us. The culture of conviviality, cohabitation and fellowship, on the other hand, is a culture that is based on service, a culture where people are open and where people get their hands dirty.

This is the gesture to keep in mind. Do you want to save yourself from the culture that makes you feel like a failure, to protect yourself from the culture of competition, from the culture of being cast off, and go on to live a happy life? Open your hands. Extend your open hands with a smile, never seated, always in movement. Get your hands dirty. You will be happy if you do.

THE TEMPTATION TO STAY WITHIN SAFE BOUNDARIES

We need a push from the Holy Spirit so that we do not become paralyzed by fear and excessively cautious, so we may venture out and not remain within safe boundaries. Let us remember that anything enclosed eventually grows musty and unhealthy. When the apostles felt that worries and dangers were paralyzing them and preventing them from venturing forth, they joined in prayer to beg for *parrhesía*: "Now, Lord, consider their threats and enable your servants to speak your word with great boldness" (Acts 4:29). The result: "After they prayed, the place where they were meeting was shaken. And they were all filled with the Holy Spirit and spoke the word of God boldly" (Acts 4:31).

Like the prophet Jonah, we are constantly tempted to flee to a safe haven. It can have many names: individualism, spiritualism, closing ourselves off in little worlds, addiction, settling down, following patterns set by others, dogmatism, nostalgia, pessimism, finding refuge in customary ways. It can be hard to leave a familiar place and way of life. The challenges we face can be like the storm, the whale, the worm that dried the gourd, or the wind and sun that burned Jonah's head. And as they were for him, so they can help us return to the God of tenderness, who wants to show us the path that constantly renews.

THE COURAGE TO MOVE FORWARD

We must have courage. Pope Paul VI used to say that he did not understand disheartened Christians. He simply did not understand them. He was referring to those sad and anxious Christians who make a person wonder if they actually believe in God or in "the goddess of lamentation." It is hard to know. These people moan and complain every single day and about every single thing: look at where the world is headed, what a disaster, what a disaster. But if you reflect on it, the world is no worse than it was five centuries ago! The world is the world; it always was the world.

Christians have to be brave. When facing a problem, we have to have the courage to move forward, to proceed bravely. And when nothing can be done, we must patiently tolerate it. Courage, tolerance and patience. Courage is moving forward, doing things, bearing witness forcefully. Tolerance is bearing the burden on our shoulders of the things that cannot be changed. We must move forward with patience, the patience given to us by grace.

But what should we do with courage, tolerance and patience? We need to step outside ourselves. We need to leave our communities and go where men and women live, work and suffer in order to proclaim the mercy of the Father who appeared to humankind in the form of Jesus Christ of Nazareth. We need to proclaim this grace, which was given to us by Jesus.

WE ARE CALLED TO DO
GREAT THINGS

Don't let others rob you of hope and joy, or drug you into becoming a slave to their interests. Dare to be more; your being is more important than any object. You do not need possessions or appearances. You can become what God, your Creator, knows you are if you realize that you are called to something greater.

Ask the Holy Spirit for help, and walk with confidence toward the great goal of holiness. In this way, you will not become a photocopy, but fully yourself.

While perusing the life of Our Lord and the saints, he began to reflect, saying to himself: "What if I should do what Saint Francis did?" "What if I should act like Saint Dominic?"...He seemed to feel a certain readiness for doing them, with no other reason except this thought: "Saint Dominic did this; I, too, will do it." "Saint Francis did this; therefore I will do it."...This succession of thoughts occupied him for a long while, those about God alternating with those about the world. But in these thoughts there was this difference. When he thought of worldly things it gave him great pleasure, but afterward he found himself dry and sad. But when he thought of journeying to Jerusalem, and of living only on herbs, and practicing austerities, he found pleasure not only while thinking of them, but also when he had ceased.

This difference he did not notice or value, until one day the eyes of his soul were opened and he began to inquire the reason of the difference. He learned by experience that one train of thought left him sad, the other joyful. This was his first reasoning on spiritual matters... When gradually he recognized the different spirits by which he was moved, one, the spirit of God, the other, the devil, and when he had gained no little spiritual light from the reading of pious books, he began to think more seriously of his past life, and how much penance he should do to expiate his past sins.

St. Ignatius of Loyola[9]

TAKE A RISK, EVEN IF IT MEANS MAKING A MISTAKE!

Do not watch life pass by. Do not confuse happiness with an armchair or live out your life behind a screen. Please do not become like the sorry sight of an abandoned vehicle! Do not be a parked car, but dream freely and make good decisions. Take risks, even if it means making mistakes. Do not go through life anesthetized or approach the world like a tourist. Make some noise! Chase away the fears that paralyze you. Do not become mummified.

Live! Dedicate yourself to living well! Open the door of your cage and fly! But, please, whatever you do, do not choose to take early retirement.

IF YOU KNOW HOW TO CRY WITH THOSE WHO CRY, YOU WILL TRULY FIND HAPPINESS

The Scriptures often speak of the feelings experienced by those who let themselves be touched viscerally by the pain of others. Jesus' own feelings made him share in other people's lives. He made their pain his own. The mother's grief became his own; the anguish of the death of her young son became his own (see Luke 7:12–15).

Young people have often shown that they are capable of *compassion*. So many of the young have generously helped out whenever situations demanded it. When there are disasters, earthquakes and floods, armies of young volunteers step up and offer a helping hand. The ways in which youth have mobilized to defend the environment is proof of their ability to hear the cry of the earth.

Do not let yourselves be robbed of this sensitivity! May you always hear the plea of those who are suffering and be moved by those who weep and die in today's world. "Some realities of life are only seen with eyes cleansed by tears."[10] If you can learn to weep with those who are weeping, you will find true happiness. So many people are disadvantaged and victims of violence and persecution. Let their wounds become your own and you will be bearers of hope in this world. You will be able to say to your brother or sister: "Arise, you are not alone." You will help them realize that God the Father loves us, that Jesus is the hand extended to help us up.

THE DEVASTATING
TENDERNESS OF GOD

You can approach the realities of pain and death that you encounter; you, like Jesus, can touch them and bring about new life. This is possible thanks to the Holy Spirit, but only if your heart has been touched by his love, if you have experienced his goodness toward you, if your heart has been warmed. If you can feel God's immense love for every living creature—especially our brothers and sisters who are hungry, thirsty, ill, unclothed or imprisoned (see Matt. 25:31–46)—then you, too, will be able to draw near to them, as he does. You will be able to touch them, as he does. You will be able to bring his life to your friends who are inwardly dead, who suffer or who have lost faith and hope.

DO NOT BE AFRAID OF PARTICIPATING
IN THE REVOLUTION OF TENDERNESS

Complaining your life away is not good! It is not good to spend your days licking your wounds. Too many people become victims of depression, alcohol and drugs! Too many elderly people live alone, with no one to share their present, ever fearful that their past will return to them.

You can respond to these challenges with your presence, by encountering others. Jesus invites us to step out of ourselves and encounter others face-to-face with boldness.

It is true that believing in Jesus often means taking a leap of blind faith, and this can be frightening. Other times, it can make us question ourselves and force us to abandon our preconceptions. This, in turn, can bring on anguish: we may be tempted by discouragement. But take courage! Following Jesus is a passionate adventure that gives meaning to our lives; it makes us feel part of a community that encourages us, a community that is always with us, which allows us to do service for others. It is deeply worthwhile to follow Christ! Do not be afraid to take part in the revolution to which he invites us: the revolution of tenderness.

WHO DO YOU IDENTIFY WITH?

Jesus tells the story of a man who was assaulted by thieves and who lay injured on the side of the road. Many people passed by, but no one stopped—people who held important social positions, yet lacked real concern for the common good. They were not willing to spend a single minute caring for the injured man, or even to call for help. Only one person stopped, approached the man, cared for him personally, took care of him and even used his own money to provide for his needs.

Above all, this man gave the injured man something that we, in our frenetic world, cling to tightly: he gave him his time. Surely this man had plans, needs, commitments and desires for that day. But he was able to put them all aside when he saw someone in need. Without even knowing the injured man, he recognized that he deserved his time and attention.

Who do you identify with? This question is blunt, direct and incisive. Who, of these figures, do you resemble? We must acknowledge that we are constantly tempted to ignore others, especially the weak. Let us admit it: for all the progress we have made, we are still illiterate when it comes to standing by, caring for and supporting the most frail and vulnerable members of our developed societies. We have become accustomed to looking the other way, to passing by and ignoring situations until they affect us directly.

BEING LIKE THE GOOD SAMARITAN

Faced with so much pain and suffering, our only course of action is to be like the Good Samaritan. Any other choice would imply that we have either joined forces with the aggressors or become like the people who walked by without showing compassion for the suffering man.

The parable of the Good Samaritan shows us how a community can be rebuilt by men and women who identify with the vulnerability of others, who reject the creation of an exclusive society and, instead, act in a neighborly way, assisting and rehabilitating those who have fallen, and doing it for the common good. At the same time, the parable makes us aware of those who think only of themselves, who fail to shoulder the inevitable responsibilities of life.

WHO WILL WE CHOOSE TO BE?

Sooner or later, along our paths, we will encounter a person who is suffering. Every day there are more of them. The decision whether to include or exclude those who lie wounded along the road informs all economic, political, social and religious plans. Every day we are faced with the choice of being either Good Samaritans or indifferent passersby.

If we take a good look at the history of the world and our own personal histories, we see that each of us is or has been like all the characters in the parable. We all have aspects of the wounded man, the aggressors, the indifferent people who passed by and the Good Samaritan.

LET US LOOK FOR OTHERS

Every day offers us new opportunities. We should not expect those who govern us to resolve everything; that would be simplistic and childish. We have the possibility of being co-responsible, of coming up with and enacting new processes and changes. We need to take an active role in aiding and supporting our troubled societies. We have ample opportunities to express our innate need for fellowship, to be Good Samaritans who bear the pain of other people's troubles rather than fomenting more hatred and resentment.

We need to share the pure and simple desire to be a unified people, a community, constantly and tirelessly seeking to include, integrate and lift up the fallen. We may often find ourselves succumbing to the mentality of the violent and blindly ambitious, those who spread mistrust and lies. Let us allow others to see politics or the economy as an arena for their own power plays. Let us foster what is good and place ourselves at its service.

We can start from the bottom and, case by case, take action at the most concrete and local levels and then expand to the farthest reaches of our countries and our world, always with the same care and concern that the Samaritan showed for each of the wounded man's injuries. Let us seek out others and embrace the world as it is, without fear of pain or a sense of inadequacy. It is there that we will discover the goodness that God has sowed in human hearts.

Difficulties that might seem overwhelming are actually

opportunities for growth, not excuses for sadness or inertia, which lead only to resignation and submission. But let us not undertake this alone, as individuals. Just as the Samaritan sought out an innkeeper who could care for the man, we are called to see ourselves as a unit that is stronger than the sum of its individual members. Indeed, let us not forget that "the whole is greater than the part, but it is also greater than the sum of its parts."[11] Let us renounce pettiness and resentment and endless confrontation. Let us stop feeling sorry for ourselves and acknowledge our crimes, apathy and lies. Reparation and reconciliation will grant us new life and will set us free from fear.

THE IMPORTANT THING IS NOT TO LIVE ONLY FOR OURSELVES

God, through Jesus, approached all men and women. He shared in the joy of the wedding at Cana in Galilee and in the anguish of the widow of Nain; he entered the house of Jairus, affected by death, and the house of Bethany, which was perfumed with nard; he took sickness and suffering upon himself and eventually gave up his life for all.

Following Christ means going to the places he did. It means taking on the burden, like the Good Samaritan, of the wounded we see along the side of the road. It means searching for the lost sheep. Being like Jesus means being with people, sharing their joys and sorrows; showing, through love, the fatherly face of God and the maternal caress of the Church.

May no one ever feel distant, detached or isolated. Each of you is called to serve our brothers and sisters by following your own gifting, be it through prayer, catechesis, teaching, caring for the sick or poor, proclaiming the Gospel or performing various works of mercy. The important thing is not to live for yourself alone. Jesus did not live for himself, but for the Father and for us.

WE ARE THE NEIGHBORS

Who is my neighbor? During Jesus' time, the word "neighbor" usually meant those closest by, those who were nearest. It was implied that help should be offered first and foremost to those who were part of one's own tribe. Among certain Judeans of that era, Samaritans were looked down upon, considered impure and not to be helped. Jesus, himself a Jew, completely upends this approach. He asks people to reconsider who their neighbors are; he asks us to be neighbors to all.

His suggestion is that we make ourselves available to those in need of help, regardless of whether or not they belong to our social group. In this case, the Samaritan *became a neighbor* to the wounded Judean. In the act of approaching and assisting, he crossed all cultural and historical barriers.

Jesus concludes the parable with an instruction: "Go and do likewise" (Luke 10:37). In other words, he challenges us to cast aside our differences and, when faced with suffering, to approach others with no questions asked. In so doing, I no longer say that I have neighbors to help, but that I must be a neighbor to others.

DO NOT BE AFRAID TO SHOW LOVE!

In this day and age, with personal relationships suffering owing to the lack of kindness being given freely, with everything for sale and graciousness hard to find, let us Christians remind people that God, in order to be our friend, asks for nothing other than to be accepted. The only thing that Jesus asks is to be accepted.

Let us reflect on those who live in desperation because they have never met anyone who showed them kindness, comforted them or made them feel precious and important. How can we, disciples of the crucified One, refuse to go to places where no one wants to go out of fear of compromising ourselves or being judged by others, and thereby denying our brethren God's Word? We need to do it freely! We have received this grace freely; we must give it freely.

Do not be afraid. Do not be afraid of love, of God our Father's love. Do not be afraid to receive the grace of Jesus Christ. Do not be afraid of the freedom that comes with the grace of Jesus Christ. Do not be afraid of grace; do not be afraid of stepping outside yourself or your Christian community to go and show love, the love of God.

We must not be afraid! Let us continue onward, explaining to our brothers and sisters how we experience the grace of Jesus, how it costs us nothing. We merely receive it! Onward!

> Yet it is not our part to master all the tides of the world, but to do what is in us for the succor of those years wherein we are set, uprooting the evil in the fields that we know, so that those who live after may have clean earth to till.
>
> J. R. R. Tolkien[12]

THE COURAGE OF GOING AGAINST THE GRAIN

We must have the courage to go against the grain. Not against someone—which is a temptation of everyday life and the typical approach of conspiracy theorists and perpetual victims, who constantly blame others. No, we need to go against the unhealthy grain of our own selfishness, closed-mindedness and rigidity, which frequently seeks to rope in others for survival. We need to go against the grain in order to become more like Jesus. He teaches us how to counter evil with only the humble and lowly force of good, without shortcuts, deceit and duplicity. Our world, beset by so many evils, does not need any further ambiguous compromises; it does not need people who waver, who go wherever the wind blows, wherever their own interests take them, who veer first to the right and then to the left, depending on which is more convenient for them. Christians who do that are like tightrope walkers, always performing balancing acts, trying to avoid getting their hands dirty, not wanting to compromise their lives and never getting seriously involved.

You must steer clear of being like that. Be free and true and conscientiously criticize society. Don't be afraid to criticize! The world needs criticism. Many people, for example, are mobilizing against environmental pollution. We need this! Criticize freely. Be passionate about truth, so that you can follow your dreams and say, "My life is not captive to the mindset of the world: I am free because I reign with Jesus in the name of justice, love and peace!" It is my hope and prayer that all people can joyfully say, "With Jesus, I too am a king." I am a king and I am a living sign of the love of God, of his compassion and tenderness.

I am a dreamer, dazzled by the light of the Gospel; I stare into the night for visions with hope. And when I fall, thanks to Jesus, I always rediscover the courage to keep fighting, hoping and dreaming. In every single phase of life.

THE COURAGE TO BE HAPPY

God calls us to make definitive choices. He has a plan for everyone. Discovering that plan and following your vocation is akin to moving toward personal fulfillment. God calls on each of us to be holy, to live his or her own life, but he has a particular path for each of us.

In today's world, which is dominated by a belief in the ephemeral and temporary, many preach the value of "enjoying the moment." They say it is not worth making lifelong commitments or strong choices or believing in "forever," simply because we do not know what tomorrow will bring. I ask you to be revolutionaries. I ask you to go against the grain. I ask you to rebel against this culture that sees everything as temporary and ultimately believes you are incapable of being responsible, and which would have you believe you are incapable of true love.

Have the courage to go against the grain. Have the courage to be happy.

PART 3

———

HAPPINESS IS A PATH

THE ART OF WALKING
WITH HUMANITY

Walking is an art. If we walk too fast, we get exhausted, and that impedes us from reaching our destination. We also fail to arrive at our destination if we stop to take rests all the time.

Walking is the art of looking to the horizon, focusing on *where* we want to go but also putting up with the fatigue that comes from walking. The journey is often difficult: "I want to stay faithful to this journey, but it is not easy...there are dark days, days of failure, sometimes I fall..."

Do not be afraid of failure; do not be afraid of falling. In the art of walking, it is not falling that matters; it is staying down. Get up quickly and resume the journey: this is walking with humanity. But do not forget that it is also terrible to have to walk alone: terrible and tedious. Walk with others, with your friends, with those who love you: this will help you reach your destination. It helps all of us.

Martina: Babette!…Oh, that was a good dinner!
  Truly excellent. Everyone thought the same thing!
Babette: I was once head chef…at the Café Anglais.
Martina: We'll all remember this evening when
  you've gone back to Paris.
Babette: I'm not going back to Paris.
Martina: You're not going back to Paris?
Babette: No one's waiting for me there. They're
  all gone…And I have no money.
Martina: No money? But the 10,000 francs?
Babette: All spent…
Martina: Ten thousand francs?
Babette: Dinner for twelve at the Café Anglais
  costs 10,000 francs.
Philippa: But dear Babette…You ought not to
  have given away all you had for our sake.
Babette: It wasn't just for your sake.
Martina: So you will be poor now all your life…
Babette: An artist is never poor.
Philippa: Was this the sort of dinner you'd
  prepare at the Café Anglais?
Babette: I could make them happy when I did my
  very best. Papin understood that.
Philippa: Achille Papin?
Babette: Yes. He'd say…"Through all the world
  there goes one long cry from the heart of the
  artist: Give me leave to do my utmost."
Philippa: But this is not the end, Babette…I feel
  certain this is not the end. In paradise you will
  be the great artist God meant you to be. Ah,
  how you will enchant the angels!
                                    Babette's Feast[1]

WE NEVER ARRIVE IF WE
TRAVEL ALONE

Don't let the world try to convince you that it is better to travel alone. On your own you will never arrive. Yes, you can achieve success in your life, but it will be without love, without companions, without belonging to a people, without that beautiful experience of undertaking a risk together. It is unthinkable to travel alone.

LIKE YOUNG CHILDREN

We are like children who continuously fall down, like toddlers trying to walk but keep falling, who need their parents to help them get up, over and over again. It is the forgiveness of the Father that helps us to our feet again: the forgiveness of God.

IF YOU FALL, GET BACK UP!

Divine forgiveness is immensely effective, because it does what it says. It does not hide the sin; it eradicates and erases it. It removes the sin at the root. It is not like sending something to the dry cleaner to have a stain removed. No! God eradicates our sins from the root. In so doing, the penitent is purified; stains are eliminated and that person is purer than snow.

With forgiveness, we sinners become new beings and are filled with spirit and joy. A new reality begins for us: we have a new heart, a renewed spirit, a new life. We—forgiven sinners, recipients of divine grace—can even teach others not to sin anymore.

"But Father, I am weak, I keep falling," they say.

And I reply, "If you fall, get to your feet again! Stand up!"

When children fall, what do they do? They reach out to their mothers and fathers so they can get back up. Let us do the same! If you fall into sin because of weakness, reach up: the Lord will take your hand and help you up. God's forgiveness gives us the dignity of helping us back up and setting us on our feet. God created men and woman to stand on two feet.

NEVER GIVE UP

Jesus gives us true passion for life. Jesus inspires us not to settle for little but to give the very best of ourselves. Jesus challenges us, spurs us on and convinces us to keep at it whenever we are tempted to give up. Jesus urges us to look upward and dream of great things.

You might say to me, "But, Father, it is so difficult to dream of doing great things; it is so difficult to rise up, to be always moving forward and upward. Father, I am weak, I fall and get up but then I fall again. It happens so many times."

Mountain climbers sing a very beautiful song when they are climbing. The words go something like this: "In the art of climbing, it's not important if you fall. What matters is that you don't stay down."

If you are weak and you fall, look up: you will see Jesus' hand reaching out to you, and you will hear him say, "Rise up and come with me."

"What if I fall again?" you ask.

Then you get to your feet again.

"What if it happens another time after that?"

You keep getting up.

Peter once asked the Lord, "Lord, how many times?"

And the reply was: "Seventy times seven" (Matt. 18:21–2, ESVUK).

Jesus' hand always reaches out to us, always ready to help us when we fall.

ONLY HE WHO DOESN'T WALK DOESN'T FALL

Jesus speaks to you, to me, to all of us throughout the Scripture when he says, "Arise."

We are well aware that even we Christians constantly fall and have to get to our feet again. Those who do not walk do not fall, but they do not move forward either. This is why we need to accept the help that Jesus offers us; we need to place our faith in God.

The first step is to let ourselves get up; the new life Jesus offers us is good and worth living because it is sustained by the One who will always be by our side as we journey to the future, helping us live life in a dignified and meaningful way.

> Endure, and conquer! Jove will soon dispose
> To future good our past and present woes.
> With me, the rocks of Scylla you have tried;
> th' inhuman Cyclops and his den defied.
> What greater ills hereafter can you bear?
> Resume your courage and dismiss your care,
> An hour will come, with pleasure to relate
> Your sorrows past, as benefits of Fate.
>
> Virgil[2]

77

GOD WALKS WITH US

For I was hungry and you gave me something to eat, I was thirsty and you gave me something to drink, I was a stranger and you invited me in, I needed clothes and you clothed me, I was ill and you looked after me, I was in prison and you came to visit me.

(Matt. 25:35–6)

Jesus' words answer the question that often echoes in our hearts and minds: where is God? Where is God if there is evil in our world, if men and women go hungry and thirsty, if there are homeless, exiles and refugees? Where is God when innocent people die as a result of violence, terrorism and war? Where is God when cruel diseases destroy the bonds of life and affection? Or when children are exploited and debased, or when they suffer from grave illnesses? Where is God when people are filled with anguish and doubt and are troubled in spirit?

Some questions do not have mortal replies. We can only look to Jesus and ask him. And Jesus' reply is, "God is in them." Jesus is in them; he suffers within them and deeply identifies with each one. He is so closely united to them that he practically forms "one body" with them.

Jesus himself chose to identify with our brothers and sisters in pain and anguish by agreeing to tread the way of sorrows that led to Calvary. By dying on the cross, he surrendered himself into the hands of the Father, assuming with self-sacrificing love the physical, moral and spiritual wounds of all humanity. By embracing the wood of the cross, Jesus embraced the nakedness, hunger, thirst, loneliness, pain and death of men and women throughout time.

AGAINST THE TIDE AND TOWARD HAPPINESS

The Word of the risen and living Lord reveals to us how to reach true beatitude, the way that leads to heaven. It is difficult to see the path because it goes against the grain, but the Lord tells us that those who travel this path are happy or become happy.

TAKING RISKS ON GRAND IDEALS

We must be magnanimous. We must be bighearted and fearless. We must always bet on grand ideals. But we must also show magnanimity toward smaller things, everyday things. It is important to find this magnanimity with Jesus, in contemplating him. Jesus opens windows on to the horizon. Magnanimity means walking with Jesus, our hearts being attentive to what Jesus tells us.

JOY IS A PILGRIM'S GIFT

Joy can't be stopped: it must move forward because it is a pilgrim's virtue. It is a gift that moves forward, which walks along the road of life, which walks with Jesus: by preaching and proclaiming the message of Jesus—joy—the road lengthens and widens. It is a virtue of the great, of those who rise above pettiness, who do not stoop to human pettiness, who always look out to the horizon.

Joy is a virtue of the path. As St. Augustine said, "Sing and keep on walking!"[3] This is Christian joy: a Christian sings with joy and sets out, bearing this joy. Even though this joy may be at times concealed by the cross, Christians sing and walk. They know how to praise God, like the apostles when they came down from the Mount, after the ascension of Jesus. Joy is the gift that leads us to the virtue of magnanimity. Christians cannot be pusillanimous: they must be magnanimous.

DO NOT BE SAD MEN AND WOMEN

Jesus is God, but he lowered himself to walk with us. He is our friend, our brother. He illuminates our path. And so the first word I wish to say to you is: *joy*! Do not be sad men and women—a Christian should never be sad—never give in to discouragement!

Our joy does not stem from having many possessions, but from having encountered a single person: Jesus, who is among us. Our joy is born from knowing that he is always with us; we are never alone, even in difficult moments, even when we encounter problems and obstacles in life that seem insurmountable! And that is when the enemy, the devil, comes to us. Often he is disguised as an angel and speaks to us slyly. But do not listen to him!

Let us follow Jesus! Not only do we accompany and follow Jesus, but we also know that he accompanies us and carries us on his shoulders. This is our joy; this is the hope that we must bring to this world. Do not let yourselves be robbed of hope!

TOGETHER WE FIND NEW STRENGTH

If we walk together, young and old, we remain firmly rooted in the present and, from here, we can revisit the past and look to the future. We revisit the past in order to learn from history and heal old wounds that at times still trouble us. We look to the future in order to nourish our enthusiasm, allow dreams to emerge, awaken prophecies and let hope blossom. Together we can learn from one another; warm hearts inspire each other with the light of the Gospel and find new strength.

DO NOT WANDER EMPTILY THROUGH LIFE

If life were a play or a video game, it would have a precise start and finish, a beginning and an end, when the curtain falls or one team wins. But life measures time differently: according to the beating of God's heart. Sometimes it passes quickly; at other times it goes slowly. At times we advance; at times we regress; sometimes we attempt new paths or change direction...

Indecision seems to come about when we fear that the curtain will fall or that time will run out, that we will not be able to advance to the next level. But life always moves forward; it never stays still. Life is always about looking for the right way, without being afraid to retrace our steps if we make a mistake.

The most dangerous thing is when our path becomes a labyrinth and we walk in circles without ever making real progress. Do not get trapped in a labyrinth! Follow a path that leads to the future. No labyrinths! Only forward movement!

THE WORD THAT FREES UP JOY

The "good news" that Jesus proclaims to the amazement of all is this: God is nearby and he wants to take care of you, me, everyone. This is the best way to describe God: nearby. That is even how he defines himself. In Deuteronomy, he says to the people, "What other nation is so great as to have their gods near them the way the LORD our God is near us whenever we pray to him?" (Deut. 4:7).

A God who is nearby, compassionate and tender wants to relieve the burdens that crush you; he wants to warm your wintry coldness, illuminate your dark days, support you when your steps falter. He does this with his Word: he rekindles hope amid the ashes of your fears, helps you rediscover joy in the labyrinths of your sorrow, fills your solitude with hope. He helps you advance, but not in a labyrinth. He helps you set out, daily, on your journey to find him.

KEEP THE FLAME OF LOVE BURNING BRIGHTLY IN YOUR EYES

The Lord does not want men and women to follow him reluctantly, without joy in their hearts. Jesus wants people who understand that being with him fills their lives with immense happiness, every day of their lives, every day anew. A disciple of God's kingdom who is not joyful does not evangelize this world. We do not become Jesus' preachers by sharpening the weapons of rhetoric: you can talk and talk and talk, but without joy...

How do we become preachers of Jesus? By keeping the sparkle of true happiness in our eyes. Frequently we see

Christians who transmit the joy of faith with their eyes. With their eyes! This is why Christians—as did the Virgin Mary—keep the flame of their love for Jesus alive.

Of course, we all encounter trials in life; there are moments when we must move forward despite the cold and crosswinds, despite much bitterness. But Christians know the way that leads to the sacred fire; it filled them with warmth once and will do so forever.

Living Flame of Love
O Living Flame of Love,
That woundest tenderly
My soul in its inmost depth!
As thou art no longer grievous,
Perfect thy work, if it be thy will,
Break the web of this sweet encounter.

How gently and how lovingly
Thou wakest in my bosom,
Where alone Thou secretly dwellest;
And in Thy sweet breathing
Full of grace and glory,
How tenderly Thou fillest me with Thy love.
St. John of the Cross[4]

BRINGING LIGHT TO THE NIGHT OF THE WORLD

You are God's present day, the today of the Church! You are not just the future; you are today. Either you start playing today, or you have lost the match. Today.

The Church needs you, so that she can be fully herself. The Church is the body of the risen Lord present in the world. I would like you to always remember that you are members of one body, this community. You are linked to one another; on your own, you will not survive. You need one another if you are to make a difference in this world, which is increasingly fragmented.

Think about this: as our world grows more and more divided, with divisions bringing wars and conflict in their wake, you must be a message of unity, a message that is worth following. Only by journeying together will we be truly strong. Together with Christ, the Bread of Life who gives us strength for the journey, let us bring the light of his fire upon the darkness of this world!

SOWERS OF HOPE

Once again, the Lord invites you to be a key figure and to serve others. He wants you to be *a concrete response* to the needs and suffering of humanity. He wants you to be signs of his merciful love in this era!

To enable you to carry out this mission, he shows you the way of personal commitment and self-sacrifice, the way of the cross. The way of the cross is the path to happiness; it will allow you to follow Jesus to the end, throughout the most trying situations of everyday life. This way does not fear failure, ostracism or solitude because it fills our hearts with the fullness of Jesus.

The way of the cross is a godly way of life; it is his "style," and it leads us into the parts of society that are fragmented, unjust and corrupt.

The way of the cross is not a sadomasochistic practice. Only the way of the cross can defeat sin, evil and death, for only it leads to the radiant light of Christ's resurrection and opens on to the horizons of a new and fuller life. It is the way of hope and the future. Those who follow it with generosity and faith give hope to the future and to humanity. Those who follow it with generosity and faith sow seeds of hope. I want you to be sowers of hope.

SET OUT TO SEA; STEP OUTSIDE YOURSELVES!

The "goddess of lamentation" is a deception: she leads you down the wrong path. When everything seems to be stagnant and at a standstill, when personal problems trouble us and social hardships do not get resolved in the way that is right, do not think of yourself as beaten.

Jesus is the way: we must get him to climb aboard our "boat" and set out with him! He is the Lord! He changes how we look at life. Faith in Jesus leads to a more far-reaching hope, to a certainty based not on our abilities and skills, but on the word of God, on his invitation. To embrace it we do not need to make endless calculations or worry about our safety measures. We need to set out to sea, go beyond our usual limits, leave our small worlds behind and open up to God, open up to our brothers and sisters. Opening up to God helps us be open with others.

Take a few steps outside yourselves—little steps, but steps nonetheless. Small steps will lead you toward God and others; they will open your hearts to community, friendship and solidarity.

"COME! FOLLOW ME!"

The very wealthy man mentioned in the Synoptic Gospels (see Matt. 19:16–22; Mark 10:17–22; Luke 18:18–23) walked, or rather ran, toward the Lord, eager to find out from the Teacher how he might inherit eternal life, which is to say, happiness.

The Gospels do not mention the man's name, which suggests that he might represent all of us. In addition to possessing great wealth, he appears to be well educated, as well as moved by a healthy need to search for true happiness and to live life fully. This is why he chooses to approach a figure of authority, someone who is believable and reliable. He finds this authority in the person of Jesus, and so poses him the question: "Good teacher...what must I do to inherit eternal life?" (Mark 10:17). But the young man asks the question as if eternal life were a possession to be acquired with his own strength.

The Lord replies with a question: "Why do you call me good?...No one is good—except God alone" (Mark 10:18). In so doing, Jesus directs him to God, who is the only and greatest Good from which comes all other goodness.

To help the man gain access to the source of goodness and true happiness, Jesus tells him the first part of the journey he must undertake, which is to learn how to do good to his neighbor. "If you want to enter life, keep the commandments"

(Matt. 19:17). By so doing, Jesus brings him back down to earthly life and indicates the path that will lead to eternal life, which is to say concrete love for his neighbor.

But the young man says that he has always done this, and he has realized that it is not enough to follow the precepts to be happy. So Jesus looks at him, with his gaze full of love (see Mark 10:21). He recognizes the desire for fulfillment that the young man carries in his heart and his healthy need to search for it; this is why he feels tenderness and affection.

Jesus, however, also realizes what the man's weak point is: he is too attached to his many possessions. So the Lord suggests a second step for him to undertake, that of passing from the logic of *deserving* to that of *giving*: "If you want to be perfect, go, sell your possessions and give to the poor, and you will have treasure in heaven" (Matt. 19:21). Jesus inverts the perspective: he invites the young man not to think about assuring himself a place in heaven, but to give up everything in this earthly life, thereby imitating the Lord. This step calls on him to go further, to go beyond following the precepts in order to attain the gift of gratuitous and total love.

Jesus asks him to leave behind that which burdens his heart and creates an obstacle to love. Jesus is not so much proposing a man who has nothing but a man who is free and rich in relationships. If the heart is crowded with possessions, the Lord and the man's neighbor will only be objects among the many. Having too much and wanting too much suffocates our hearts; it makes us unhappy and incapable of loving.

Finally, Jesus suggests a third step, that of imitation: "Come, follow me" (Matt. 19:21).

Following Christ is not a loss, but an incalculable profit; renunciation pertains to losing the obstacles that lie in the path of love. The heart of that young man, however, is divided between two masters: God and money. The fear of risking and losing his possessions makes him go home sad: "At this the man's face fell. He went away sad, because he had great wealth" (Mark 10:22). While he had not been afraid of asking the decisive question, he did not have the courage to accept the reply, which was to untie himself from himself and his wealth and tie himself to Christ, to walk with him and discover true happiness.

Friends, to all of you Jesus says, "Come! Follow me!" Have the courage to live by trusting in the Lord and setting out on the path with him. Let yourselves be won over by his loving gaze that frees us from idolatrous seduction, from those false riches that promise life but lead to death. Do not be afraid of welcoming the Word of Christ and accepting his call.

LET US NOT CLOSE OURSELVES OFF IN OUR LITTLE WORLDS

Always be sure to choose the right path. What does that mean? It means knowing how to journey through life and not wander aimlessly without a clear destination.

What do you do? Do you journey or wander? Our lives are not without direction. Life has a clear goal, and it was given to us by God. He guides us and gives us direction through his grace. It's as if he has placed software inside us that allows us to discern his divine program and answer him with freedom. But, like all software, it also needs to be constantly updated. Keep your program updated, listen to the Lord and accept the challenge to do his will. It is sad when the software is not updated. It is even sadder when it is broken and does not work.

The only thing that gives us direction and helps us move forward on the right path is *knowledge born of faith*. This is not the false knowledge offered to us by this world we live in. To receive knowledge born of faith we need to observe the world, our situations and our problems through the eyes of God. We receive this knowledge when we begin to see things with the eyes of God, to listen to others with the ears of God, to love with the heart of God and to appreciate things with the values of God.

This knowledge helps us understand and reject *false promises of happiness*. There are so many! A culture that makes false promises can never free its people; it can only lead to selfishness that fills the heart with darkness and bitterness. The knowledge of God, however, helps us understand how to accept those who act and think differently from the way we do.

It is sad when we begin to close ourselves off in our little worlds and listen only to ourselves. It is like saying, "My way or the highway." It is a bad principle. When we adopt this principle we remain entrapped, closed in on ourselves. When a people, a religion or a society becomes "a small world," it loses the best it has and takes on a presumptuous mentality that says, "I am good and you are bad." The knowledge of God opens us up to others. It helps us look beyond our own personal comforts and the false securities that make us blind to the great ideals that make life even more beautiful and worthy of being lived.

ALWAYS GO BEYOND

The joy of the Gospel that brings happiness to a community of disciples is a missionary joy. The seventy-two disciples felt it as they returned from their mission (see Luke 10:17). Jesus felt it when he rejoiced in the Holy Spirit and praised the Father for revealing himself to the poor and the little ones (see Luke 10:21). It was felt by the first converts who marveled to hear the apostles preaching because "each one heard their own language being spoken" on the day of Pentecost (Acts 2:6).

This joy is a sign that the Gospel has been proclaimed and is bearing fruit. Yet the drive to go forth and give, to step outside ourselves, to keep journeying and sowing, remains ever present. The Lord says, "Let us go somewhere else—to the nearby villages—so that I can preach there also. That is why I have come" (Mark 1:38). Once the seed has been sown in one place, Jesus does not remain behind to explain things or to perform additional signs; the Spirit moves him to go forth to other towns.

SETTING OUT ON A JOURNEY

Before they could worship the child in Bethlehem, the Magi had to undertake a lengthy journey. Matthew tells us that in those days "Magi from the east came to Jerusalem and asked 'Where is one who has been born king of the Jews? We saw his star when it rose and have come to worship him'" (Matt. 2:1–2).

A journey always involves a transformation, a change. After a journey, we are no longer the same as we once were. There is always something new about those who have taken a journey: they have learned new things, encountered new people and situations, and have found inner strength from the hardships and risks they met along the way. No one worships the Lord without first experiencing the interior growth that comes from taking a journey.

LET US CHOOSE THE ROAD OF GOODNESS

What does it mean to travel toward the Lord? It means taking the path of goodness, not of evil; the path of forgiveness, not of vengeance; the path of peace, not of war; the path of solidarity, not of selfishness.

WHERE IS MY HEART DIRECTED?

Lent is *a journey back to God*. How many times, either when we were too active or else indifferent, have we said to him, "Lord, I will come back to you, but later, in a bit…I can't today but tomorrow I will start to pray and do something to help others."

We do this over and over. But God speaks to our hearts now. We will always have things to do in life, we will always find excuses to offer, but, my brothers and sisters, now is the time to go back to God.

"Come back to me," he says, "*with all your heart*." Lent is a journey that involves our whole life, our entire being. It is a time for rethinking the path we are on, for finding the route that leads us home so that we can rediscover our profound relationship with God, on whom everything depends.

Lent is not just about making sacrifices. It is a time for discerning where our hearts are directed. This is the core of Lent. We need to ask ourselves: where are our hearts directed? Let us ask: where is my life's navigation system taking me—toward God or toward myself? Do I live to please the Lord, or to be noticed, praised, put at the head of the line? Do I have an unsteady heart, one that wobbles this way and that, forward and then back? Do I love the Lord for a short while and then go back to worldly ways? Or is my heart steadfast in God? Am I comfortable with my hypocrisy, or do I work to free my heart from the duplicity and falsehood that tie it down?

The journey of Lent is *an exodus that takes us from being enslaved to being free.* These forty days correspond to the forty years that God's people trekked through the desert to return to their homeland. How difficult it was to leave Egypt! During their journey, they were constantly tempted to return; they clung to memories of the past and to various idols. So it is with us: our journey back to God is blocked by our unhealthy attachments, held back by the seductive appeal of sins, by the false security of money and appearances, by the paralysis of our discontentment. To embark on the journey, we have to cast off these illusions.

> *Il Matto*: I'm not well educated but I have read a couple of books. You might not believe me but everything that exists in this world serves a purpose. Take that stone there, for example.
> *Gelsomina*: What purpose does it have?
> *Il Matto*: It's for ... What do I know? If I knew, you know who I'd be?
> *Gelsomina*: Who?

Il Matto: Almighty God, who knows everything, when you're born, when you die. Who can possibly know all that? No, I don't know what that stone is for, but it has to have a purpose because if it's useless, then everything is useless. Even the stars. That's what I think. You, too. You have to have a purpose, you, and your cabbage head.

La Strada[5]

STAY THE COURSE

In order to stay the course of our journey, let us stand in front of the cross of Jesus: it is the silent throne of God. Every day let us contemplate his wounds, the wounds that he carried to heaven and shows every day to the Father in his prayer of intercession. Let us contemplate these wounds every single day.

In those gashes, we can see our own emptiness, our shortcomings, the wounds our sins have provoked and the hurt we have suffered. We also see how God does not point his finger at us, but opens his arms to embrace us. His wounds were inflicted for our sake, and because of those wounds we have been healed (see 1 Pet. 2:22–5; Isa. 53:5). By kissing those wounds, we come to realize that God awaits us with infinite mercy in life's most painful traumas. It is there, where we are most vulnerable, where we feel the most shame, that he came toward us. And having come toward us, he now invites us to return to him and rediscover the joy of being loved.

Bless and sanctify my soul with heavenly benediction, so that it may become Your holy dwelling and the seat of Your eternal glory. And in this temple of Your dignity let nothing be found that might offend Your majesty. In Your great goodness, and in the multitude of Your mercies, look upon me and listen to the prayer of Your poor servant exiled from You in the region of the shadow of death. Protect and preserve the soul of Your poor servant among the many dangers of this corruptible life, and direct him by Your accompanying grace, through the ways of peace, to the land of everlasting light.

Thomas à Kempis[6]

THE FINAL HORIZON OF OUR PATH

The final pages of the Bible show us the ultimate horizon of our journey as believers: the new Jerusalem, the celestial Jerusalem. It is chiefly described as an immense dwelling, where God will welcome all of humankind so as to dwell with them definitively (see Rev. 21:3). This is our hope.

And what will God do when we are with him at last? He will show us infinite tenderness, like a father who welcomes home his children after they have toiled greatly and suffered.

WE WILL CRY, YES, BUT WITH JOY

Jesus Christ leads us to the great "dwelling" of God with humankind, with all our brothers and sisters; we will bring God the memory of our days lived here on earth. It will be lovely to discover that nothing will have been lost—not a smile or a tear. However long our life will have been, it will feel like one breath.

Creation did not stop on the sixth day of Genesis, but continues tirelessly, because God is always looking after us. He continues to do so until the day of fulfillment, until that morning when tears will fade away, and then God will pronounce his final word of blessing: "Behold," the Lord will say, "I am making everything new" (Rev. 21:5). Yes, our Father is the God of newness and surprise. And on that day we will be truly happy and we will weep. We will weep tears of joy.

TONIGHT, IF YOU FEEL AN HOUR OF DARKNESS IN YOUR HEART

Dear sister, dear brother, if you experience an hour of darkness tonight for a day that has not yet dawned, a light that has dimmed or a dream that has shattered, go, open your heart with awe to the message of Easter: "Do not be afraid. He has risen! You will see him in Galilee" (see Matt. 28:5–7). Your expectations will not remain unfulfilled, your tears will be dried, your fears will be replaced by hope. For, as you know, the Lord always precedes you; he always walks ahead of you. And with him, life always begins anew.

Holy Sonnet X

Death, be not proud, though some have called
    thee
Mighty and dreadful, for thou art not so;
For those whom thou think'st thou dost
    overthrow
Die not, poor Death, nor yet canst thou kill me.
From rest and sleep, which but thy pictures be,
Much pleasure; then from thee much more must
    flow,
And soonest our best men with thee do go,
Rest of their bones, and soul's delivery.
Thou art slave to fate, chance, kings, and
    desperate men,
And dost with poison, war, and sickness dwell,
And poppy or charms can make us sleep as well
And better than thy stroke; why swell'st thou
    then?
One short sleep past, we wake eternally
And death shall be no more; Death, thou shalt die.

John Donne[7]

FROM FEAR TO MARVEL

The women thought they would find a body to anoint; instead, they found an empty tomb. They had gone to mourn the dead; instead, they heard a proclamation of life. For this reason, the Gospel tells us, "Trembling and bewildered, the women went out and fled the tomb" (Mark 16:8). They were filled with fear and bewilderment. Bewilderment, which in this case was fear mixed with joy, came over their hearts when they saw that the great stone before the tomb had been rolled away and inside was a young man in a white robe. It was wonder at hearing the words, "Don't be alarmed . . . You are looking for Jesus the Nazarene, who was crucified. He has risen!" (Mark 16:6). And then they received his message: "He is going ahead of you into Galilee. There you will see him" (Mark 16:7).

Let us also accept his invitation, for it is the *message of Easter*. Let us go to Galilee, where the risen Lord awaits us.

LET YOURSELVES BE SURPRISED BY FAITH

Going to Galilee means *setting out on new paths*. It means walking away from the tomb. The women went looking for Jesus in the tomb; they went in remembrance of what they had experienced with him, which was now gone forever. They went to experience their grief.

This is an image of faith as the recollection of something that was once beautiful and which now can only be recalled. This kind of faith is formed of habits, things of the past, wonderful childhood memories, which no longer affect or challenge us. Going to Galilee, on the other hand, means realizing that faith, if it is alive, must get back on the road. Our faith needs to feel new; it needs to feel like the first days of the journey, with all the amazement of our first encounter. And then we need to trust in it, not thinking that we know everything, but always having the humility of someone who allows themselves to be surprised by God's ways. Often we are afraid of God's surprises! Often we are worried that God will surprise us. But today the Lord invites us to let ourselves be surprised. Let us go to Galilee, then, and discover that God cannot be filed away among childhood memories, but that he is alive and filled with surprises. Jesus rose from the dead; Jesus never ceases to amaze us.

Faith is not an album of memories; Jesus is not an outdated figure. He *is alive here and now*. He walks beside you every day. He is in every situation you are experiencing, in every trial you have to endure, in your deepest hopes and dreams. He forges new paths where you least expect them. He urges you to go against the grain and not have regrets or be jaded. Even if you feel that all is lost, allow yourself to be bewildered by his newness: he will surely surprise you.

REDISCOVER THE GRACE OF DAILY LIFE

Going to Galilee also means *going to the margins*. Galilee was a distant place: the people who lived in that diverse and disparate region were far away from the ritual purity of Jerusalem. But that is where Jesus began his mission; he directed his message to people who were struggling to get by: the excluded, vulnerable and poor. He brought them the face and presence of God, who tirelessly seeks out those who are discouraged or lost in the margins of existence, since in his eyes no one is lost, no one is excluded.

The risen Lord continues to ask his disciples to go there, even now. He asks us to go to Galilee, to the real "Galilee" of daily life, to go out into the streets we walk along every day, to the intersections in our cities. The Lord precedes us. He makes himself felt in the lives of those around us, the people who share our days, homes, jobs, our difficulties and hopes. We discover that in Galilee we can find the risen One in the faces of our brothers and sisters, in the enthusiasm of those who dream, in the resignation of those who are discouraged, in the smiles of those who rejoice and in the tears of those who suffer. Above all, the latter: the poor and those on the fringes. We will be amazed by how the greatness of God is revealed in little things, how his beauty shines forth in the poor and simple.

Jesus, the risen Lord, loves us without boundaries and is present in every moment of our lives. He made himself present in the heart of our world. He invites us to overcome barriers, banish prejudices and stand by those near us in our everyday lives; in so doing we will rediscover the *grace of everyday life*. Let us recognize him here in our very own Galilee, in everyday life. With him, life will change. The risen One lives beyond all defeats, evil and violence, beyond all suffering and death, and guides history.

LIFE CAN ALWAYS BEGIN AGAIN WITHIN US

Above all, going to Galilee means *starting over*. For the disciples it meant going back to the place where the Lord first sought them out and called them to follow him. This was the place of their first encounter, where they first loved Jesus. From that moment on, after casting aside their nets, they followed Jesus, listening to his preaching and witnessing the miracles he performed. And yet, even though they were always with him, sometimes they did not fully understand him. Frequently they misunderstood his words, and, when they stood at the foot of the cross, they fled and left him alone.

Despite this failure, the risen Lord once more appears in Galilee as the One who precedes them. He is always ahead of them. He is standing before them and calling them to follow him, saying, "Let us start over from the beginning. Let us begin anew. I want you to be with me again, in spite of everything." In this Galilee, we learn to be amazed by the Lord's infinite love, which opens new roads into the paths of our failure. This is how the Lord is: he creates new roads along the paths of our failures. This is how he is; he invites us to Galilee to do this.

It is always possible to begin again: God can always awaken new life in us, despite all our failures. From the rubble in our hearts—we all have rubble in our hearts—God can create a work of art. From the ruined remnants of our humanity, God can make new history. He never ceases to precede us: on the cross of suffering, in desolation and in death, as in the glory of a life that rises again, in a changing history, in a hope that is reborn.

PART 4

HAPPINESS IS NOT JUST GETTING BY

THAT WHICH IS EPHEMERAL
AND THAT WHICH ENDURES

God alone can give our life the fullness we so deeply desire and which is so difficult to attain. So many people, in our day and age, purport to be dispensers of happiness: they promise us swift success, great profits, magical solutions to all our problems and so on. How easy it is to slip unwittingly into sinning against the first Commandment: idolatry, substituting God with an idol. Idolatry and idols might seem like they are from another age, but in reality they are of *all* ages! Even today. The presence of idols in our society explains certain contemporary attitudes far better than many sociological studies.

This is why Jesus opens our eyes to reality. We are called to happiness, to be blessed, and we become so to the extent that we place ourselves on the side of God, his kingdom, on the side of not that which is ephemeral but that which endures eternally.

We are happy when we acknowledge before God that we are needy—and this is very important—when we say, "Lord, I need you"—and then, like him and with him, we stand by the poor, the suffering and the hungry. We, too, in the face of God are poor, afflicted and hungry. Although we possess worldly goods, we experience joy not when we idolize others or sell our souls, but when we are able to share with our brothers and sisters.

SUPERFICIAL PLEASURES

The great danger in today's world, pervaded as it is by consumerism, is the desolation and anguish born of a complacent yet covetous heart that leads to the feverish pursuit of frivolous pleasures and a blunted conscience. Whenever our interior life becomes caught up in its own interests and concerns, there is no longer room for others, no place for the poor. God's voice is no longer heard, the quiet joy of his love is no longer felt, and the desire to do good fades.

This is a very real danger for believers, too. Many fall prey to it and end up resentful, angry and listless. This is no way to live a dignified and fulfilled life. This is not God's will for us, nor is it the life of the Spirit, which has its source in the heart of the risen Christ.

PURITY, KINDNESS, MERCY

Choosing purity, meekness and mercy; choosing to entrust oneself to the Lord despite our poverty and affliction; dedicating oneself to justice and peace: these are all ways of going against the grain with respect to the mindset of the contemporary world and its culture of possession, meaningless entertainment and arrogance against the weak.

God's Grandeur
The world is charged with the grandeur of God.
 It will flame out, like shining from shook foil;
 It gathers to a greatness, like the ooze of oil
Crushed. Why do men then now not reck his rod?
Generations have trod, have trod, have trod;
 And all is seared with trade; bleared,
  smeared with toil;
 And wears man's smudge and shares
  man's smell: the soil
Is bare now, nor can foot feel, being shod.

And for all this, nature is never spent;
 There lives the dearest freshness deep down things;
And though the last lights off the black West went
 Oh, morning, at the brown brink eastward,
  springs—
Because the Holy Ghost over the bent
 World broods with warm breast and with ah!
  bright wings.
        Gerard Manley Hopkins[1]

THE COURAGE OF SIMPLICITY

First of all, try to be *free with regard to material things*. The Lord asks us to assume a lifestyle that is marked by simplicity by refusing to yield to the culture of consumerism. This means focusing on the essentials and learning to do without all those suffocating extras. Let us learn to step away from the frenzy of possessing, from the idolatry of money and lavish spending. Let us put Jesus first. He can free us from the kinds of idol worship that enslave us.

Put your trust in God, dear young friends! He knows and loves us; he never forgets us. Just as he provides for the flowers in the field (see Matt. 6:28), so he will make sure that we lack for nothing. If we are to come through the financial crisis, we must be ready to change our lifestyles and stop being wasteful. Just as we need the courage to be happy, we also need the courage to live simply.

THE COURAGE OF FREEDOM

Be free! Some people may think that freedom means doing whatever one wants, seeing how far one can go, pushing the limits, overcoming boredom. This is not freedom. Freedom means being able to think about our actions, being able to judge good and bad, discerning what kinds of conduct lead to our development; freedom means always choosing to do good.

Let us be free in the name of goodness. And in this let us not be afraid to go against the grain, even if it is not easy! Being free to choose goodness is demanding but it will make us people of conviction, people who can face life, people who have courage and patience.

WATCH OUT FOR SNAKE OIL SELLERS

The Beatitudes of Jesus (see Matt 5:3–12) are a decisive message that urges us not to place our trust in material and fleeting things, not to seek happiness by following snake oil vendors—who often peddle death—and con artists. We should not follow them because they can never give us hope.

The Lord helps us open our eyes so we can see reality more clearly and heal the chronic short-sightedness with which the worldly spirit infects us. With his paradoxical Word, he is able to stir us and enable us to recognize that which truly enriches us, satisfies us and gives us joy and dignity; in other words, what truly gives meaning and fullness to our lives.

WE ARE IN THIS WORLD TO HAVE THE AUDACITY TO MAKE STRONG CHOICES

When you dream of love, don't go looking for "special effects" but remember that each of you is special, each one of you. Every single one of us is a gift and we can each make our own life into a gift. Other people await you: your communities, the poor.

Dream of a beauty that goes beyond appearances, beyond cosmetics, beyond trends and fads. Dream fearlessly of creating a family, of having children and raising them well, of spending your life with another person and sharing everything. Don't be ashamed of your faults and flaws, for there is someone out there ready to accept and love them, someone who will love you just as you are. This is love: loving someone as he or she is.

Our dreams reveal the kind of life we want. Great dreams are not about powerful cars, fashionable clothes or wild vacations. Do not listen to those who appeal to your dreams but actually peddle illusions. Dreaming is one thing; having illusions is another. Those who peddle illusions by speaking about dreams *manipulate your happiness*. We were created for a much greater joy: each of us is unique and was put into this world to be loved for who we are, and to love others in our own unique and special way.

Life is not a game where we sit on the bench waiting to be called in to substitute someone else. No, each of us is unique in God's eyes. Do not let yourselves be "standardized" or turned into a nameless piece on an assembly line. None of us is "standard issue." We are all unique, free and alive, called to live a love story with God, to make bold and firm decisions, to accept the marvelous risk of loving.

THE RICH HEART AND THE POOR HEART

The Gospel invites us to peer into the depths of our heart to see where we find security. Often, the rich experience security through their wealth: they think that if their wealth is threatened, the meaning of their earthly life is on the verge of collapse. Jesus tells us this in the parable of the rich fool. He speaks of a man who was sure of himself and yet foolish, for it did not dawn on him that he might die that very day (see Luke 12:16–21).

Wealth ensures nothing. Indeed, when our hearts feel rich, we become so self-satisfied that we leave no room for God's Word, for the love of our brothers and sisters or for enjoying the most important things in life. In this way, we miss out on the greatest treasure of all. This is why Jesus calls blessed those who are poor in spirit (see Matt. 5:3), those who have a poor heart, for there the Lord can enter with his perennial newness.

SHROUDS DON'T HAVE POCKETS!

We cannot serve two masters: God and money (see Luke 16:13). As long as humankind seeks to accumulate wealth for themselves, there will never be justice. Instead, by entrusting ourselves to God's providence and seeking his kingdom together, no one will lack the means to live with dignity.

A heart that is filled with the desire for possessions is a full heart, but empty of God. This is why, in the Bible, Jesus frequently warns the rich; they place their security in the material goods of this world, when ultimate security can only be found in God. In a heart possessed by wealth, there is not much room for faith as everything is focused on wealth. If, however, one gives God his rightful place, which is to say the primary place, his love will lead a person to share their wealth, to place it at the service of projects of solidarity and development. This has often happened in the history of the Church, and even in recent times. In so doing, God's providence is delivered through our service to others, through sharing.

When someone does not keep wealth for themselves but places it in the service of others, in an act of solidarity, the providence of God is made visible. What will happen to someone who accumulates wealth only for themselves when they are called to God? That person will not be able to take their riches with them, because shrouds do not have pockets!

It is better to share, for we take with us to heaven only what we have shared with others.

AN OBSESSIVE SEARCH FOR WEALTH LEADS TO UNHAPPINESS

God is not a distant and anonymous being. He is our refuge, the wellspring of our peace and tranquility. He is the rock of our salvation, to which we can cling with the certainty of not falling. One who clings to God never falls! He is our defense against ever-lurking evil. God is a great friend, ally and Father to us, but we do not always realize it. We do not realize that we have a friend, an ally, a Father who loves us; we prefer to rely on immediate goods that we can touch, on contingent goods, forgetting and at times rejecting the supreme good, which is the paternal love of God. Remembering that he is our Father, in this epoch of orphanhood, is so important!

We distance ourselves from God's love when we search incessantly for earthly goods and riches, thus demonstrating an exaggerated preference for these realities. Jesus tells us that this frenetic search is illusory and causes unhappiness. He gives his disciples a fundamental rule of life: "Seek first his kingdom and his righteousness" (Matt. 6:33). It is a matter of fulfilling the plan that Jesus proclaimed in the Sermon on the Mount. We need to entrust ourselves to God (for God does not disappoint—friends, or people we thought were friends, have disappointed us but God never disappoints!) and dedicate ourselves to the faithful stewardship of the goods that he has given us, including earthly goods, but in moderation, without overdoing it, without behaving as if everything, including our salvation, depends only on us.

This evangelical attitude requires a clear choice, which the Gospel of Luke indicates clearly: "You cannot serve both God and Money" (Luke 16:13). You can choose either the Lord or fascinating but illusory idols. This choice has an impact on many of our actions, plans and commitments. It is a choice that needs to be made and continually renewed, because the temptation to reduce everything to money, pleasure and power is relentless.

While honoring idols might lead to tangible, albeit fleeting, results, choosing God and his kingdom does not always immediately bear fruit. It is a decision made with hope, and we leave its complete fulfillment to God. Christian hope goes beyond; it does not stop when faced with difficulty because it is founded on God's faithfulness, which never fails. He is faithful. He is a faithful Father, friend, ally.

BEAUTY BEYOND APPEARANCES

There is beauty in a laborer who returns home grimy and unkempt but feeling the joy of having earned food for their family. There is extraordinary beauty in the unity of a family gathered around a table, generously sharing what food it has, even if it is simple fare. There is beauty in a wife, slightly disheveled and no longer young, who continues to care for her sick husband despite her own failing health. Long after the springtime of their courtship has passed, there is beauty in the elderly couple who still respect and love one another deeply in the autumn of their lives, who still hold hands when they take a walk.

There is also a kind of beauty, unrelated to appearances or fashion, in those men and women who pursue their personal vocations with love, who selflessly give service for their community or nation, who work hard to build a family, who toil to advance social harmony. Finding, showing and highlighting this beauty, which reminds us of Christ on the cross, is a way of laying down a foundation for genuine social solidarity and the culture of encounter.

SPENDING YOUR LIFE IN FRONT OF THE MIRROR IS AN UGLY THING

Do not give in to the temptation of concentrating only on yourself, on navel-gazing, becoming selfish or superficial when faced with sorrow, difficulties or even fleeting success. Let us remember that what happens to others can also happen to us. Let us go against the tide of individualism, which isolates us, makes us egocentric and vain, concerned only with our image and well-being. It is ugly to spend your life in front of the mirror.

LAUGH AT YOURSELVES

Young narcissists stand in front of the mirror and comb their hair over and over... Allow me to give you some advice: now and then, when you look in the mirror, laugh at yourself. Laugh at yourself! It will do you good.

EMPTY THRILLS

It grieves me to meet young people who seem to have opted for "early retirement." Young people who seem to have retired at the age of twenty-three, twenty-four or twenty-five. I worry when I see young people who have thrown in the towel before the game has even begun, who have given up even before they begin to play. I am saddened to see young people walking around glumly as if life has no meaning.

It is also difficult, as well as troubling, to see young people waste their lives looking for empty thrills, following dark paths in order to feel more alive, which they end up paying for in the end... and dearly. So many young people have chosen this path, surely you know some. It is disturbing to see young people squandering some of the best years of their lives, wasting their energy by chasing after people who peddle false illusions (who exist in great numbers), who in turn end up robbing them of their strengths. Young people who follow these illusions experience a kind of vertigo, their heads spin and they end up with nothing.

All this grieves me deeply.

THE OPPOSITE OF A BANAL LIFE

Often, in this day and age, people live mediocre and dull lives, probably because they have never tried searching for true treasure. They are content with attractive but fleeting things, glittering flashes that actually prove to be illusory and reveal only darkness. The light of the kingdom is not like fireworks. Fireworks last only an instant, but the light of the kingdom accompanies us throughout our lives.

The kingdom of heaven is the opposite of the superfluous things that the world offers us. It is the opposite of a dull life. It is a treasure that renews life every day and leads us toward wider horizons. Indeed, those who have found this treasure have creative and inquisitive hearts, hearts that do not repeat things emptily but constantly invent and find new paths that lead us to love God, to love others and to truly love ourselves. The sign of those who walk this path of the kingdom is creativity. Creativity is a force that takes life and then gives and gives and gives... Creativity constantly looks for ways to give life.

Jesus, who is both a hidden treasure and a pearl of great value (see Matt. 13:44–6), inspires joy; he inspires all the joy in the world: the joy of discovering the meaning of life and the joy of feeling committed to the adventure of holiness.

THE BEAUTY OF SIMPLICITY

Hedonism and consumerism can be sneaky. In our search for pleasure, we end up becoming far too concerned about ourselves and our right to have the free time we crave to enjoy ourselves. If we do not cultivate a certain simplicity of life and resist the feverish demands of a consumer society, which ultimately leave us feeling impoverished and unsatisfied, anxious only to attain everything immediately, it is unlikely we will feel and show any real concern for those in need. Similarly, if we let ourselves get caught up by social media and other rapid forms of communication and virtual reality, we become dazed and indifferent to the suffering flesh of our brothers and sisters.

And yet, amid this whirlwind of activity, we continue to hear the Gospel, which offers us the promise of a different life—a healthier and happier one

BE VIGILANT

Be alert. Do not get distracted. Stay awake! Being vigilant means not letting our hearts become lazy or our spiritual life relax into mediocrity. Be careful because it is easy to become "sleepy Christians." We all know many such Christians, people who are anesthetized by society; Christians without spiritual fervor, who do not pray with intensity, who merely repeat the words of prayer like a parrot; Christians who lack enthusiasm for the mission, who have no passion for the Gospel; Christians who are incapable of looking to the horizon. All this leads to "snoozing," allowing things to move forward by inertia alone, falling into apathy, remaining indifferent to everything except that which is comfortable. This is a sad life, and there is no happiness there.

EMPTY THRILLS OR FULFILLMENT?

We do not want to be robbed of the best of ourselves, our energy, our joy or our dreams, all because of false hopes. Dear friends, I ask you: are you looking for empty thrills in life, or do you want to feel a power that can give you a lasting sense of life and fulfillment?

Empty thrills or the power of grace? What do you want: empty thrills or fulfillment? There is a way of gaining new life, one that is not for sale, which cannot be purchased. This way is not a thing or an object, but a person. His name is Jesus Christ. I ask you: can you buy Jesus Christ? Is Jesus Christ for sale at the shops? Jesus Christ is a gift, a gift from the Father, *the* gift from our Father.

FREEDOM IS CHOOSING GOODNESS

Many people will tell you that freedom means being able to do whatever you want. But you need to know how to refute this. If you do not know how to refute this, you are not free. Freedom is not always getting to do what we want: this closes us off, makes us aloof, prevents us from being open and sincere friends. The "feeling fine, doing fine" approach is false. Freedom is the gift of *being able to choose goodness*: this is true freedom. A person who is free chooses what is good, which is pleasing to God, even if it requires effort, even if it is not easy.

Only courageous and strong decisions will help us make our greatest dreams, the ones that require a lifetime commitment, come true. Courageous and strong choices. Do not be content with mediocrity, with merely "getting by," with sitting down and getting comfy. Do not trust those who try to distract you from the real treasure—*you*—by telling you that life is beautiful only if you have many possessions. Be skeptical of those who would have you believe that you are only important if you act tough, like heroes in films, or if you wear the latest fashions. Your happiness has no price and cannot be bought. It is not an app that you can download on your phone; not even the latest update can bring you freedom and grandeur in love. True freedom is something else altogether.

Love is *a free gift* which calls for an open heart. Love is *a responsibility*, but *a beautiful one*, and it lasts your whole life. Love is *a daily task* for those who can achieve great dreams! Woe to young people who do not know how to dream, who do not dare to dream! If a young person cannot dream, it means they have already gone into retirement. This is not good. Love is nurtured by trust, respect and forgiveness. Love does not happen because we talk about it; it happens when we live it. It is not a romantic poem to study and memorize, but a life choice to put into practice!

HUNGER AND THIRST FOR JUSTICE

"Blessed are those who hunger and thirst for righteousness, for they will be filled" (Matt. 5:6). Yes, those who have a strong sense of justice—not only toward others, but toward themselves first of all—will be filled, because they are ready to receive the greatest justice, which only God can give.

THE TERRIBLE TRAP

I ask you in the name of the Son of God, who while fighting sin never turned away a sinner, do not fall into the terrible trap of thinking that life depends on money alone and that, in comparison with money, everything else is devoid of value or dignity. This is nothing but an illusion! We cannot take money with us into the life beyond. Money does not bring us true happiness. Violence inflicted for the sake of amassing riches that are soaked in blood makes one neither powerful nor immortal. Everyone, sooner or later, will be subject to God's judgment. No one can escape that.

Now is the moment to change your life! Now is the moment to allow our hearts to be touched! When faced with evil deeds, even in the face of serious crimes, now is the time to listen to the cry of innocent people who are deprived of their property, dignity, feelings and their very lives. Staying on the path of evil leads only to illusions and sadness. True life is something entirely different. God never tires of reaching out to us. He is always ready to listen.

THREE KINDS OF DESTITUTION

Destitution is poverty without faith, support or hope. There are three types of destitution: material, moral and spiritual.

Material destitution is what is normally called poverty; it affects those living in conditions that run counter to human dignity: those who lack basic rights and needs such as food, water, hygiene, work and the opportunity to develop and grow culturally. In response to this destitution, the Church offers help (*diakonia*) to meet these needs and to bind the wounds that disfigure the face of humanity. In the poor and outcast we see Christ's face; by loving and helping the poor, we love and serve Christ. Our efforts are also directed toward ending violations of human dignity, discrimination and abuse in the world, for these are often the cause of destitution. When power, luxury and money become idols, they take priority over the need for a fair distribution of wealth. Our consciences need to be converted to justice, equality, simplicity and sharing.

No less a concern is *moral destitution*, which consists in becoming enslaved to vice and sin. How much pain families experience because one of their members is a slave to alcohol, drugs, gambling or pornography. How many people no longer see meaning in life or prospects for the future and have lost hope. How many are plunged into destitution by unjust social conditions or unemployment, which takes away their dignity as breadwinners, or by lack of equal access to education and health care. In these cases, moral destitution is not unlike impending suicide.

This type of destitution, which also causes financial ruin, is invariably linked to the *spiritual destitution* we experience when we turn away from God and reject his love. If we think we do not need God, who reaches out to us through Christ, because we believe we can get by on our own, we are headed for a fall. God alone can truly save and free us.

THE WEALTH OF POVERTY

We need to wholeheartedly follow the Lord's invitation to "repent and believe the good news" (Mark 1:15). This *conversion* consists primarily in opening our hearts, recognizing the many different forms of poverty and manifesting the kingdom of God through a lifestyle consistent with the faith we profess. Often the poor are viewed as a group of people unto themselves, a "category" in need of specific charitable services. Following Jesus means changing this particular way of thinking, embracing the challenge of sharing and getting involved.

Christian discipleship is not about accumulating earthly treasures, which give the illusion of security but are actually fragile and fleeting. On the contrary, it requires a willingness to be set free from all that holds us back from achieving true happiness and bliss, so that we can recognize what is lasting, what cannot be destroyed by anyone or anything (see Matt. 6:19–20).

Here, too, Jesus' teaching goes against the grain, for it promises what can only be seen through the eyes of faith and with absolute certainty. "And everyone who has left houses or brothers or sisters or father or mother or wife or children or fields for my sake will receive a hundred times as much and will inherit eternal life" (Matt. 19:29). Unless we choose to become poor in ephemeral wealth, worldly power and vanity, we will never be able to give our lives in love; we will live a fragmented existence, full of good intentions but ineffective at transforming the world. We need, therefore, to open up to the grace of Christ, which can make us witnesses to his boundless charity and give meaning and credibility to our presence in the world.

REFUSE ALL COMPROMISES

Compromises with the world are dangerous. Christians are always tempted to make compromises with the world, with the spirit of the world. Rejecting compromises and following the way of Jesus Christ is the life of the kingdom of heaven; it is the greatest joy and true happiness.

> The glory of a good man is the testimony of a good conscience. Therefore, keep your conscience good and you will always enjoy happiness, for a good conscience can bear a great deal and can bring joy even in the midst of adversity. But an evil conscience is ever restive and fearful.
>
> Sweet shall be your rest if your heart does not reproach you.
>
> Do not rejoice unless you have done well. Sinners never experience true interior joy or peace, for "there is no peace to the wicked," says the Lord.
>
> Thomas à Kempis[2]

TRUTH WITHIN US

If I were in Pilate's place, if I had to look Jesus in the eye, what would I be ashamed of? Faced with the truth of Jesus, the truth that is Jesus, in what ways am I deceitful or duplicitous? How do I displease him?

Each of us has such ways. We need to look for them, seek them out. We all have these duplicities, these compromises; we shuffle things around so that the cross seems farther away. It is good to stand before Jesus, who is truth, so we can be set free from our illusions. It is good to worship Jesus so that we can be inwardly free, so that we can see life as it really is and not be deceived by the fashions of the moment and the displays of consumerism that dazzle but also deaden. We mustn't let ourselves be enchanted by the sirens of the world; we need to take our lives in hand and take a bite out of life in order to live it to the fullest!

A SOCIETY WITH NO HEART

Let us not remain indifferent and silent in response to God's call.

We need to consider the countenance we want our society to have and think about how we value human life. We need to remember that the progress of people cannot be measured by technological or economic advances alone. We need to be open to being moved, to respond to those who arrive on our doorstep, whose expressions discredit and debunk all the false idols that try to take over and enslave us, idols that promise illusory and momentary happiness but have little to do with the reality and suffering of others. How arid and inhospitable a city becomes when it loses the capacity for compassion! Such is a heartless society.

WORDS ARE NOT ENOUGH

Let us reflect on someone who lives without hope, someone who is steeped in profound sadness from which they are struggling to emerge, someone who thinks they have found happiness in alcohol, drugs, gambling, the power of money or excessive sexuality...only to find themselves even more disappointed, now and then venting their rage against life with violence in a way that is unworthy of humanity.

How many sad people there are! And they all lack hope! Think of the many people who, after trying so many things, fail to find meaning in life and look to suicide as a solution. Why do they do this? Because they have not found hope. They have tried so many things, but society, which is cruel, cannot give them hope.

Hope is like grace: it cannot be bought; it is a gift of God. We must offer Christian hope as our witness, with freedom and joy. The gift of grace that God offers us brings hope. We who realize we are not orphans, who know we have a Father, cannot remain indifferent.

But how can we offer hope? By walking up and down the streets and saying, "I have hope"? No! We must do it by bearing witness, with our smile.

The Word without bearing witness is merely air. Words alone are not enough.

DO YOU NEED LOVE?

Each and every day, ask the Holy Spirit to help you experience the great message anew. No? Why not? You have nothing to lose. He can change your life, fill it with light and lead it down a better path. He will not hinder you; he will help you find everything you need, and in the best possible way.

Do you need love? You will not find it in outrageous acts, by using people, by trying to be possessive or domineering. You will find it in a way that will make you genuinely happy.

Do you seek powerful emotions? You will not experience them by accumulating material objects, spending money, chasing desperately after things. Powerful emotions will come to you, and in a much more beautiful and meaningful way, if you let yourself be moved by the Holy Spirit.

THE ILLNESS OF PESSIMISM

You will say to me: but the world does not think like that; the world thinks differently. We talk a lot about love but, in reality, another principle is at work: *people are only concerned about themselves.*

Do not let this fact, or any of the other things that are not right, including the evil that is everywhere, condition you. Do not let yourself be imprisoned by the sadness, resignation and discouragement of those who say that nothing will ever change. Once you start believing that, you, too, will fall ill with pessimism.

Have you ever seen the face of a pessimistic young person? Have you seen the expression on their face? They look embittered, disappointed. Pessimism makes us ill with bitterness, it ages us from within, it makes us age faster.

So many disruptive forces are at work these days, so many people spread blame everywhere and on everyone: these professional complainers disseminate negativity. Don't listen to them! Complaints and pessimism are not Christian. The Lord detests glumness and victimhood. We were not made to look down at the ground, but to raise our eyes toward heaven, to look at others and to society.

GET BACK UP!

"Arise!" This is the first step of the mission and I invite you to reflect on it. Jesus gives us the strength to get to our feet and to steer clear of the death of focusing solely on ourselves, of the paralysis of egoism, laziness and superficiality.

We see these kinds of paralysis everywhere. They impede us from moving forward and living a strong faith and oblige us to live out a faith that is museum-like, more dead than alive. Jesus, to resolve this ugly attitude, says, "Arise!" so that we can move toward a future that is alive and filled with hope and charity toward our brethren. The mission begins when we start to take the word of the Lord Jesus seriously: Arise again!

THE VOICE OF GOD AND
THE VOICE OF EVIL

There is the voice of God, which speaks kindly to the conscience, and there is the voice of temptation, which leads to evil. How can we differentiate between the voice of the Good

Shepherd from that of the thief? How can we distinguish God's inspiration from the evil one's intimations?

We can learn how to discern these two voices. They speak two different languages; they have opposite ways of knocking on the door of our hearts. Just as we know how to distinguish one language from another, we can also distinguish the voice of God from the voice of the evil one. The voice of God never forces us. God *offers* himself; he does not *impose* himself. Instead, the evil voice seduces, assails, forces. It arouses dazzling illusions and emotions that are tempting but transient. At first it flatters and makes us believe that we are all-powerful, but then it leaves us empty inside and accuses us of being worthless. The voice of God, meanwhile, patiently corrects us but also encourages and consoles us: it nourishes hope. God's voice has a horizon, whereas the voice of the evil one leads us to a wall and backs us into a corner.

Another difference: the voice of the enemy distracts us from the present and wants us to focus on fears related to the future or on sadness stemming from the past. The enemy does not want the present. His voice brings bitterness to the surface, reminding us of wrongs that have been done to us and those who have hurt us. On the other hand, the voice of God speaks in the present, and says things like, "Now you can do good, now you can use the creativity of love, now you can forego the regrets and remorse that hold your heart captive." God's voice inspires us, leads us forward and speaks to us about the present.

The two voices also raise different questions. God's voice has us ask, "What is good for me?" But the tempter will urge us to ask, "What do I feel like doing?" What do *I* feel like doing? The evil voice always revolves around the ego, its impulses and its needs, and it wants *everything immediately*.

It is like a child's tantrum: everything, right now. The voice of God, meanwhile, never promises us joy at a low price: it invites us to go beyond our ego in order to find true and good peace.

Let us never forget: evil never brings peace. First it causes us frenzy and then it leaves us with bitterness. This is the style of evil.

Lastly, God's voice and that of the tempter speak through different milieus. The enemy chooses darkness, falsehood and gossip while the Lord loves sunlight, truth and sincere transparency. The enemy will say, "Shut yourself in, no one understands you or listens to you anyway, so don't trust anyone!" Goodness, on the contrary, invites us to open up, to be clear and to trust in God and in others.

Dear brothers and sisters, we may at this time be tempted to turn inward. Let us pay attention to the voices that reach our hearts. Let us ask ourselves where they come from. Let us ask for the grace to recognize and follow the voice of the Good Shepherd, who brings us out of the enclosure of selfishness and leads us to the pastures of true freedom.

> The world is indeed full of peril, and in it there are many dark places; but still there is much that is fair, and though in all lands love is now mingled with grief, it grows perhaps the greater.
>
> J. R. R. Tolkien[3]

THE DEVIL WITH THE KIND EYES

Jesus successfully counters the draw of evil. How does he do it? He responds to temptations with the Word of God, which says that we should not take advantage of or use God, others and things for ourselves; we should not take advantage of our own position to gain privileges (see Matt. 4:1–10). True happiness and freedom do not reside in possessing but in sharing; they do not come from taking advantage of others but from loving others; they do not come from obsessing over power but in joyfully doing service.

These temptations accompany us on the journey of life. We must not be afraid of the temptations; we must remain vigilant because the temptations often appear cloaked in the form of goodness.

This is what the devil does: he arrives with gentle eyes, an angelic face; he even knows how to disguise himself with seemingly sacred and religious motives! If we give in to his flattery, we end up justifying our falsehood by disguising it with good intentions. For instance, how often have we heard people say, "Sure, some of my deals have been crooked, but I have helped the poor." Or else, "Sure, I have taken advantage of my role (as politician, governor, priest, bishop), but always in the name of good." Or else, "It's true, I gave in, it just happened, but I didn't hurt anyone." And so on, one justification after another.

Please: never compromise with evil! Do not engage in dialogue with the devil! We must not enter into dialogue with temptation; we must not let our conscience doze off, so that we also say, "It's not that bad and, besides, everyone does it!" Let us raise our eyes and look at Jesus: he does not seek compromises; he does not make agreements with evil. He opposes the devil with the Word of God, which is stronger than the devil, and thus he overcomes temptation.

REJECTING EVIL

Rejecting evil means saying "no" to temptation, sin and Satan. More concretely, it means saying "no" to a culture of death that manifests itself in escaping from reality toward a false happiness that is expressed through lies, deceit, injustice and despising others. We say "no" to all this. The new life given to us in baptism has the Spirit as its wellspring; it rejects all behaviors dominated by feelings of division and discord. This is why the apostle Paul urges us, "Get rid of all bitterness, rage and anger, brawling and slander, along with every form of malice" (Eph. 4:31). These six vices unsettle the joy of the Holy Spirit, poison the heart and lead us to curse God and our neighbors.

CLING TO THAT WHICH IS GOOD

It is not enough to refrain from doing evil in order to be a good Christian. It is necessary to *cling to that which is good* and to do good. St. Paul says, "Be kind and compassionate to one another, forgiving each other, just as in Christ God forgave you" (Eph. 4:32).

Sometimes we overhear people say, "But I never hurt anyone!" These people think they are saints. While it is fine to think that, they need to ask themselves if they also do good. Many people do not do evil, but nor do they do any good. They live their lives with indifference, apathy and mediocrity. "It is well not to do evil, but it is very evil not to do good," St. Alberto Hurtado used to say.[4]

Today, I urge you to promote good! Promote good. Do not feel that all is well when you refrain from doing evil; we are all guilty of not doing the good things we could do. It is not enough to refrain from hate; we must forgive. It is not enough to refrain from bearing grudges; we must pray for our enemies. It is not enough to refrain from causing division; we must bring peace where there is none. It is not enough to refrain from speaking ill of others; we must interrupt others when we hear them speaking badly about someone. We need to interrupt the gossiping—this is doing good. If we do not stand up to evil, we are complicit in nurturing it. It is necessary to step in wherever evil spreads. Evil spreads in the absence of bold Christians who oppose it with good, people who "live a life of love," as St. Paul says (Eph. 5:2).

PURIFY YOUR HEART FROM THE LIES THAT SULLY IT

Jesus drove out the moneychangers and all the vendors and buyers from the Temple in Jerusalem. Why did he take such forceful and provocative action? He did it because the heavenly Father sent him to cleanse the Temple: not only the Temple of stone, but also, and especially, the temples of our hearts. Just as Jesus could not stand seeing his Father's house become a marketplace, he does not want our hearts to become places of turmoil, chaos and confusion.

Our hearts must be cleansed, tidied and purified. But cleansed of what? Of the falsehoods that stain it, the hypocritical duplicity. All of us have them. They are diseases that harm the heart, soil our lives and make us insincere. We need to be cleansed of the deceptive securities that seek to barter our faith in God with passing things, bringing only temporary gains. We need the nefarious temptation of power and money to be swept from our hearts and from the Church. But to cleanse our hearts, we need to dirty our hands, we need to feel accountable and not simply look on while our brothers and sisters are suffering. How do we purify our hearts? On our own we cannot. We need Jesus. He has the power to conquer evil, heal our diseases and rebuild the temples of our hearts.

FAILURES ARE GOOD

How do I look at things? When I look at things, do I look carefully, or is it like when I quickly scroll through the thousands of photos or social profiles on my mobile phone? How often we end up being eyewitnesses to events without ever truly experiencing them! Sometimes our first reaction is to take a picture with our phone without even bothering to look into the eyes of the people involved.

All around us, but often also within us, we see death: it can be physical, spiritual, emotional or social. But do we really see this death or do we simply let it happen and just experience the consequences? Is there anything we can do to restore life?

Some people, for example, stake everything on the present moment and risk their own lives by undertaking extreme experiences. Some young people are "dead" because they have lost hope. Once a young woman told me, "My friends do not want to get involved anymore, they no longer have the courage to rise up." Sadly, depression is spreading among young people, and often it leads to the temptation to take their own lives. There are also many situations where apathy reigns, where people are plunged into an abyss of anguish and remorse! How many young people cry out with no one around to hear their plea! Instead, they are met with looks of indifference by people who are too busy enjoying "happy hour," happily keeping their distance.

Other people waste their lives on superficial things, thinking they are alive while in fact they are dead within. Already by the age of twenty, many are intent on dragging their lives down, instead of raising them up with the dignity they deserve. Everything gets reduced to "living it up," seeking out morsels of gratification: a party here, some attention there, a little bit of affection...

And then there's the growing digital narcissism that affects young people and adults alike. So many people engage in this! Some of them might have been brought up on materialism, the people around them only concerned with making money and living easy, as if that were the sole purpose of life. In the long run, this will lead to unhappiness, apathy and a boredom with life that will grow ever more frustrating.

Negative situations can also be the result of personal failure, when something we care about, something we were committed to, does not work out or give the desired results. This can happen at school or in the world of sports or in the arts. The end of a "dream" can make us feel dead. But failures are part of what it means to be human; sometimes they are even a grace! Often, something we thought would bring us happiness proves to be an illusion or an idol. Idols demand everything from us, enslaving us but giving us nothing in return. And in the end they collapse, leaving only a cloud of dust. If failure causes our idols to collapse, however, it is a good thing, even if it makes us suffer.

GOD WANTS US TO BE CONNECTED TO LIFE

For love to be fruitful, don't forget your *roots*. What are your roots? Your parents, of course, but especially your grandparents. Yes, your grandparents. They prepared the soil in which you have grown. Cultivate your roots, visit your grandparents; it will do you good. Ask them questions, take time to listen to their stories.

Today, there is a danger of growing up rootless, because we are always in a rush, on the go; everything needs to be done quickly. What we see on the internet comes into our homes immediately: just one click and people and things pop up on our screen. The risk is that those faces end up becoming more familiar than our own family members. Bombarded by virtual messages, we risk losing our real roots.

Becoming disconnected from life, existing in a fantasy world—these are not good things. They are a temptation from the evil one. God wants us to be firmly grounded, *connected to life*. He does not want us to be closed off; he wants us to always be open to others! Grounded and open.

SHAKE THE TORPOR FROM YOUR SOUL

We need to be vigilant so that our daily life does not become routine and, as Jesus says, so that we are not burdened by life's anxieties (see Luke 12:22–31). Let us therefore ask: what weighs heavily on my heart? What weighs on my spirit? What makes me want to stay lazily sitting down? It is sad to see Christians always sitting down in their comfortable chairs. What mediocrities paralyze me? What vices crush me to the ground and prevent me from looking up? And what about the burdens that weigh heavily on the shoulders of our brothers and sisters? Am I aware of them or indifferent to them?

These are good questions to ask ourselves because they help guard our hearts against apathy. "But, Father, tell us, what is apathy?" you might ask. It is a great enemy of the spiritual life and the Christian life. Apathy is a type of laziness that makes us slide into sadness; it takes away our zest for life and the will to do things. It is a negative spirit that traps the soul and robs it of its joy. It starts with sadness and slides downward so that there is no joy. The book of Proverbs says, "Above all else, guard your heart, for everything you do flows from it" (Prov. 4:23). Guard your heart! Stay vigilant!

John 1:14
The oriental histories tell a tale
Of a bored king in ancient times who, fraught
With tedium and splendor, went uncaught
And secretly around the slums to sail
Amid the crowds and lose himself in their
Peasant rough hands, their humble obscure names;
Today, like that Muslim Harum, Emeer
Of the true faithful, God decides to claim
His place on earth, born of a mother in
A lineage that will dissolve in bones, And the
    whole world will have its origin
With him: air, water, bread, mornings, stones,
Lily. But soon the blood of martyrdom,
The curse, the heavy spikes, the beams. Then numb.

Jorge Luis Borges[5]

AN INEXTINGUISHABLE
DESIRE FOR HAPPINESS

If you allow the deepest aspirations of your hearts to be expressed, you will realize that you possess an unquenchable thirst for happiness: this will allow you to debunk and reject the many "special offers" that surround you.

When our goal is only success, pleasure and the accumulation of possessions, and when we turn these into idols, we may indeed experience moments of exhilaration and an illusory sense of satisfaction, but ultimately we become enslaved, never satisfied, always looking for more. It is a tragic thing to see a young person who "has everything" but who is also weary and weak.

St. John, when writing to young people, said, "You are strong, and the word of God lives in you, and you have overcome the evil one" (1 John 2:14). Young people who choose Christ are strong: they are nurtured by his Word and do not need to stuff themselves with other things!

Have the courage to go against the grain. Have the courage to be truly happy! Say no to ephemeral, superficial, throwaway culture, for it presumes you are incapable of taking on responsibility and facing the great challenges of life.

BE THE PROTAGONISTS OF YOUR LIFE

Our memories should not be crammed together as in the memory of a hard drive. Nor can we archive everything in some sort of virtual "cloud." We need to learn how to transform past events into a dynamic reality that will give us cause for reflection, from which we can extract lessons and meaning for the present and the future. This is no easy task, but one that is necessary for seeing how the thread of God's love runs through our entire life.

Many people say that young people are distracted and superficial. I do not agree! Still, we do need to acknowledge that in our day and age we need to relearn how to reflect on our lives and direct them toward the future. *Having a past* is not the same as having *history*. We might have many *memories*, but how many of them are really a part of our *memory*? How many of them are meaningful for our hearts and help give meaning to our lives? We see faces of young people on social media in all sorts of pictures, indicating more or less *real* events, but we don't know how much of this is *truly real*, as experiences can be endowed with other purposes and meanings. Television is full of so-called "reality shows" which are not real at all. They are just moments spent in front of a television camera by characters who live from day to day, without a greater plan. Do not let yourself be led astray by this false image of reality! Be the protagonist of your history and decide your own future!

PART 5

HAPPINESS IS MAKING YOUR DREAMS COME TRUE

GOD COMES TO US AT NIGHT

God comes to us in the night of our lives, when dark clouds gather. We all know such moments. We need to be able to see him, to look beyond the night, to lift our eyes up and see him amid the gloom.

Look deep into the night! What do I mean by this? I mean let your eyes remain bright even in the darkness. Never stop seeking the light despite the darkness you may feel in your heart or see around you. Lift your gaze from the earth toward heaven, not in order to flee but to overcome the temptation to remain trapped by your own fears. This is the danger: that we will be governed by our fears.

Do not remain shut in on yourself and your complaints. Look up! Get up! This is what the Lord asks of us: Look up! Get up!

This might be the hardest task, but it will be the most exciting one. Stand tall while everything around you seems to collapse. Be a sentinel, ready to see the light in the dark night.

Be a builder amid the ruins that surround you. Allow yourself to dream. This is the key, for me. A young person who is unable to dream has grown old before their time!

A person who is capable of dreaming does not merely sit in the dark. They light a candle, a flame of hope that announces the coming of the dawn. Dream! Do it now. Look to the future with courage.

WHAT IS THE DREAM OF LIFE?

Everyone dreams of finding fulfillment. It is right that we nurture great hopes and lofty aspirations that ephemeral goals—such as success, money and entertainment—cannot satisfy. If we were to ask people to express their life's dream in one word, it would not be difficult to imagine the answer: "Love." Love gives meaning to life because it reveals life's mystery. Indeed, we only *have* life if we *give* it; we truly possess it only if we generously give it away.

I Love You
Your hands are my caress
my daily reminders
I love you because your hands
work hard for justice

Your eyes are my lucky charm
against the bad days
I love you for your gaze
that watches and seeds the future

I love you in my paradise
by which I mean my country
where the people live happily
even if they have no time off

If I love you it's because you are
my love my accomplice my all
and out in the street arm in arm
we are much more than two

Mario Benedetti[1]

THE OPPOSITE OF "I" IS "WE"

The Bible tells us that *great dreams* are the ones that can be fruitful, those that sow peace, cohesion and joy. These are great dreams because they rely on humanity as a collective.

Once, a priest asked me what the opposite of "I" is.

Naively, I fell into the trap and replied that the opposite of "I" is "you."

He corrected me by saying, "No, Father: that is the seed of war. The opposite of 'I' is 'we.'"

By saying that the opposite of "I" is "you," I create war; if I say that the opposite of "I" is "we," I build community, I make peace and friendship, and shift away from selfishness.

Great dreams include people, they involve people, they rally people together to move; they share and create new life.

To remain great, these dreams need a constant source of hope; they need to be filled with the sense of the infinite so they can expand. Great dreams need God so they do not become mirages or delusions of grandeur. You can dream great things but it is dangerous to do them on your own; they may turn into delusions of grandeur. Never be afraid to dream with God. Move forward. Dream big.

LET'S NOT LIMIT OUR HORIZONS

Let us not ignore our *great dreams*. Let us not settle only for what is necessary. The Lord does not want us to narrow our horizons or remain parked on the side of the road of life. He wants us to race boldly and joyfully toward lofty goals. We were not created to dream only about holidays or weekends, but to make God's dreams come true in this world.

God made us capable of dreaming so that we can embrace the beauty of life. The great works of mercy are the most beautiful aspects of life. They go right to the heart of our greatest dreams. If you dream about real glory, not the glory of this passing world but the glory of God, follow this path. Read the Gospel of Matthew (see especially Matt. 25:34–40) and reflect on it, for the works of mercy give glory to God more than anything else. Let me repeat that: the works of mercy give glory to God more than anything else. In the end, we will be judged on our works of mercy.

The Fountain
How well I know that flowing spring
in black of night.

The eternal fountain is unseen.
How well I know where she has been
   in black of night.

I do not know her origin.
None. Yet in her all things begin
   in black of night.

I know that nothing is so fair
and earth and firmament drink there
   in black of night.

Her shining never has a blur;
I know that all light comes from her
   in black of night.

St. John of the Cross[2]

IF WE CHOOSE TO LOVE
WE WILL BE HAPPY

How do we start to make great dreams come true? With *great choices*. The Gospel also speaks of this. Indeed, on Judgment Day, the Lord will judge us on the choices we have made. The Gospel says that he will separate the people who gather in front of him the way a shepherd divides sheep from the goats (Matt. 25:32–3). But he does not judge us; our own actions decide if we are good or evil. He only points out the consequences of our choices. He holds them up to the light and respects them.

Life, therefore, is the time for making strong, decisive,

eternal choices. Trivial choices lead to a trivial life; great choices to a life of greatness. Indeed, we become what we choose, for better or worse. If we choose to steal, we become thieves. If we choose to think of ourselves, we become self-centered. If we choose to hate, we become angry. If we choose to spend hours on our phone, we become addicted. If we choose God, we grow in his love daily. If we choose to love others, we find true happiness. *The beauty of our choices depends on love.* Do not forget this. Jesus knows that if we are self-absorbed and show indifference, we remain paralyzed, but if we give ourselves to others, we become free. We possess life only by giving it away. The Lord of life gives us the secret—which is also a rule—of life. We possess life, now and for all eternity, only by giving it away.

LET US NOT HANG ON TO THE WHYS OF LIFE

It is true that obstacles exist that can make our choices difficult: we experience fear and insecurity, and we have so many "why" questions that go unanswered. So many whys. Love, however, asks us to go beyond, to leave behind the whys of life and wait, instead, for answers to come to us from heaven.

The answer has come: it is the gaze of the Father who loves us and who has sent us his Son. Love compels us to go beyond the *why* and instead ask *for whom*, to go from asking, "Why am I alive?" to, "Whom might I live for?" To go from, "Why is this happening to me?" to, "Whom might I help?"

Whom can we help? Let us ask this! And not think only of ourselves! Life is already full of choices we make for ourselves: what to study, who to become friends with, what home to buy, what interests or hobbies we can pursue. We can waste years thinking about ourselves without ever actually starting to love. To this end, Alessandro Manzoni offers a good piece of advice: "We ought to aim rather at doing well, than being well; and thus we should come, in the end, even to be better."[3]

Not only doubts and questions can undermine great and generous choices. Other obstacles appear in our path every day. Feverish consumerism can overwhelm our hearts with superfluous things. An obsession with pleasure sometimes seems like the only way to escape problems, when it simply postpones them. A fixation on our rights and privileges leads us to neglect our responsibilities to others.

Then there is the great misunderstanding about love, which, more than a set of strong emotions, is primarily a gift, a choice and a sacrifice. The art of choosing well, especially today, means not following trends, not being standardized, not letting ourselves fall into a consumerist mentality that discourages originality, not giving into the cult of appearances. Choosing life means resisting throwaway culture and the desire to have everything now so that we can direct our lives toward heaven, toward God's dreams. To choose life is to live. We were born to live, not just to get by.

Every single day, in our heart, we face many choices. I would like to give you a piece of advice to help train you to choose well. If we look within, we often notice two very different questions rising up inside us. One asks, "What do I feel like doing?" This question often proves misleading, since it suggests that what really counts is thinking about ourselves and indulging in our wishes and impulses. The question that the Holy Spirit plants in our hearts is a very different one: not, "What do I feel like doing?" but, "What would be good for me?" This is the choice we have to make on a daily basis: should I do what I feel like doing or should I do what is best for me? This inner discernment will allow you to step away from making frivolous choices and instead make decisions that will shape your lives—it all depends on you.

Let us look to Jesus and ask him for the courage to choose what is best for us, to enable us to follow him in the way of love. In so doing, we can find joy. We can live, not just get by.

> Man, so long as he is in this world, is like a sick person lying upon a bed more or less uncomfortable, who sees around him other beds nicely made to outward appearance, smooth, and level, and fancies that they must be most comfortable resting-places. He succeeds in making an exchange; but scarcely is he placed in another, before he begins, as he presses it down, to feel in one place a sharp point pricking him, in another a hard lump: in short, we come to almost the same story over again. And for this reason, adds he, we ought to aim rather at doing well, than being well; and thus we should come, in the end, even to be better.
>
> Alessandro Manzoni[4]

DO NOT BE AFRAID OF TAKING RISKS, BUT RATHER OF LIVING LIFE IN A STATE OF PARALYSIS

We need to follow the path of our dreams. But be careful of giving in to the temptation of anxiety, for it can hold us back.

Anxiety can work against us by making us give up whenever we do not see instant results. Our best dreams are only attained through hope, patience and commitment, never in haste.

We should also be careful not to get blocked by insecurity; we should not be afraid of taking chances or making mistakes. On the contrary, we should be afraid of stasis, of becoming like the living dead, who are afraid of taking risks, making mistakes and persevering. Even if you make a mistake, you can always get up and start over. No one has the right to rob you of hope.

MAKE YOUR DREAMS YOUR FUTURE

Dreams are important. They allow us to see far and wide; they help us embrace the horizon and cultivate hope in everyday actions.

The dreams of young people are the most important of all. A young person who cannot dream is as if anesthetized; he or she cannot understand life, the power of life. Dreams revive you, they carry you far, they are like the most luminous stars, the ones that indicate a different path for humanity.

You all have brilliant stars inside you: they are your dreams. They are your responsibility and your treasure. Make them also your future! This is the task ahead of you: transform today's dreams into the reality of the future. It takes courage. When faced with resistance or difficulties, show courage. Do not let your dreams become extinguished.

BE WARY OF DREAMS THAT PUT YOU TO SLEEP

Dreams are to be nurtured, purified, put to the test and shared. But have you ever asked where your dreams come from? Where do my dreams come from? Did they come to me from watching television? Or from listening to a friend? Or from daydreaming? Are they big dreams or small ones? Are they meager dreams, happy with little? Are they comfortable dreams, related only to my well-being?

"No, I'm happy as I am. I don't want to go any further." Dreams like that won't lead you to achieve grand things! They will cause a state of death-in-life! Those are dreams of comfort, ease, dreams that lull young people to sleep, which turn courageous young people into couch potatoes.

A CRAZY MAN NAMED FRANCIS

Young people's dreams often frighten adults. Perhaps this is because the adults themselves have stopped dreaming and taking risks. Such things happen in life. Perhaps the adults are scared because the dreams of the young make them question their own choices. Or perhaps because people who dream go far. Do not let anyone steal your dreams.

Once there was a young man who, when he was around twenty years old, started having big dreams. His father, a successful businessman, tried to convince him to let them go, but he said, "No, I want to follow the dreams that I have inside." In the end, he left to follow his dream. His father tried to stop him. But the young man took refuge in a bishop's house, took off his elegant clothes and gave them to the priest. "Let me go on my path," he said.

This young man, who lived in thirteenth-century Italy, was named Francis; he changed the history of Italy. Francis risked everything to follow his big dreams. He was a young man! But how he dreamed! They said he was crazy because of his dreams. And yet he did so much good that continues to be felt today.

OFFER UP YOUR DREAMS

Never stop dreaming. And teach others how to dream. Dreams are a great strength.

"Father, where can I buy pills that will make me dream?" you ask.

No, no pills! They will not make you dream; they will lull the heart to sleep! They burn your neurons. They ruin your life.

"Well, then, where can I buy dreams?"

Dreams cannot be bought. Dreams are a gift, a gift from God, a gift that God sows in your heart. Dreams are given to us freely, so that we may give them freely to others. Offer up your dreams: you will not be any poorer if someone takes them. Offer them up freely to others.

ARTISANS OF HOPE

What better adrenaline exists than working daily, with dedication, to become artisans of dreams, artisans of hope? Dreaming helps us keep alive the certainty that another world is indeed possible, a world that we can be involved in, one that we can help build through our work, efforts and actions.

WHERE THERE ARE NO DREAMS, THERE IS UNHAPPINESS AND RESIGNATION

One of the major problems that young people have today is that they have lost their ability to dream. It is not that they dream too much or too little; they simply do not dream. And when someone does not dream, when a young person does not dream, that empty space gets filled with complaints and a sense of hopelessness or sadness. This is why it is impossible for a person to dream too much.

DEFEND YOUR DREAMS

Start dreaming and dream of everything you possibly can. I think of the words from a famous song by Modugno: *Nel blu dipinto di blu, felice di stare lassù* (literally translated as "In the Blue-Painted Blue. Happy to be up there").[5] Dream like that: boldly, unashamedly. Dream! Dream is the key word. And be ready to defend your dreams as if they were your children. This might be difficult to understand but it is easy to feel: when you have dreams, you might not know how to talk about them, but you protect and defend them so the world will not take them away.

The two facts which attract almost every normal person to children are, first, that they are very serious, and, secondly, that they are in consequence very happy. They are jolly with the completeness which is possible only in the absence of humor. The most unfathomable schools and sages have never attained to the gravity which dwells in the eyes of a baby of three months old. It is the gravity of astonishment at the universe, and astonishment at the universe is not mysticism, but a transcendent common-sense. The fascination of children lies in this: that with each of them all things are remade, and the universe is put again upon its trial. As we walk the streets and see below us those delightful bulbous heads, three times too big for the body, which mark these human mush-rooms, we ought always primarily to remember that within every one of these heads there is a new universe, as new as it was on the seventh day of crea-tion. In each of those orbs there is a new system of stars, new grass, new cities, a new sea.

There is always in the healthy mind an obscure prompting that religion teaches us rather to dig than to climb; that if we could once understand the common clay of earth we should understand everything. Similarly, we have the sentiment that if we could destroy custom at a blow and see the stars as a child sees them, we should need no other apocalypse.

G. K. Chesterton[6]

WE NEED THE ARDOR OF YOUTH

I would like to tell our young people something. We, all of us, are grateful to you when you dream.

"Really?" you ask me. "Because when young people dream, sometimes they make noise…"

So make noise! Your noise is the fruit of your dreams. When you make Jesus your life's dream, when you embrace him with joy and contagious enthusiasm, it means you do not wish to live in the dark of night. This is good for us, too! Thank you for working courageously to make your dreams come true, for believing in the light even in dark times, for committing to making our world more beautiful and humane. Thank you for all the times you cultivate the dream of unity, when you take care of God's creation, when you fight to ensure respect for the dignity of the vulnerable, for when you spread the spirit of solidarity and sharing. Above all, thank you for not losing the ability to dream in a world that thinks only of immediate gains, a world that tends to stifle grand ideals!

Do not live your lives in numbness or asleep. Instead, dream and live. It helps those of us who are older, and the Church, too. Yes, even the Church needs to dream! We need the enthusiasm of youth to be witnesses of the God who is always young!

ON OUR OWN WE RISK SEEING MIRAGES

How important it is to dream together! Please, dream together, and not by yourselves. *Always dream with others; never against others!* By yourselves, you risk seeing mirages, seeing things that are not there. Dreams are built together.

LET US CULTIVATE HEALTHY UTOPIAS

Let us not give credence to embittered and unhappy people; let us not listen to those who cynically say we should not bother cultivating hope; let us not trust those who crush youthful enthusiasm when they say that no undertaking is worth sacrificing one's whole life; let us not listen to those who are "old" at heart and stifle youthful euphoria.

Let us go to the elderly whose eyes sparkle with hope! Let us cultivate healthy utopias: God wants us to be able to dream like him and with him. He wants us to be conscientious toward reality. He wants us to dream of a different world. And if one dream is extinguished, let us dream a new one.

FELLOWSHIP OF HUMANITY, A DREAM THAT CAN COME TRUE

We are not alone. God has drawn near to us. Not with words, but through his very presence. In Jesus, God became incarnate. Because of Jesus, who became our brother, we see a brother in all men and a sister in all women. This universal communion inspires us, as a faithful community, to cooperate readily with everyone for the common good: without limits, exclusions or prejudices.

As Christians, we are called to love without borders and limits; we are called to be a sign and witness that it is possible to go beyond the walls of selfishness and personal and national interest. We can go beyond the power of money that too often decides the destiny of people. We can go beyond the divisive fences of ideology that incite hatred. We can go beyond all historical and cultural barriers and, above all, beyond indifference, the culture of indifference that we encounter every day.

We can be brothers and sisters to all; we must think and work like brothers and sisters to all. This may seem like an unrealistic utopia. But we prefer to believe that it is a feasible dream, one that can come true. For it is the dream of the triune God. With his help, it is a dream that can begin to take shape even in our world.

> *Brotherhood*
> I am a man: little do I last
> and the night is enormous.
> But I look up:
> the stars write.
> Unknowing I understand:
> I too am written,
> and at this very moment
> someone spells me out.
>
> Octavio Paz[7]

PART 6

HAPPINESS IS REVOLUTIONARY

THE MAP OF THE CHRISTIAN LIFE

In the Gospel, Jesus addresses his followers—that is, all of us—by calling us "Blessed" (Matt. 5:3). It is with this word that he begins his sermon, or "gospel," which means "good news," because it is the path toward happiness. Those who are with Jesus are blessed; they are happy. Happiness is not based on having something or becoming someone. No. True happiness is being with the Lord and living for love.

The ingredients for a happy life are called "Beatitudes": blessed are the simple and the humble, those who make room for God and are able to weep for others and for their own mistakes; those who remain meek, fight for justice and are merciful to all; those who safeguard purity of heart, who always work for peace and abide in joy, who do not hate and, even when suffering, respond to evil with good.

These are the Beatitudes. They do not require grand gestures; they are not intended for superheroes but for people who live the trials and toils of every day. They are for us. Saints are like everyone else: they breathe in the air that is polluted by evil, but they never stray from Jesus' roadmap, which is spelled out in the Beatitudes, the map of Christian life.

THE BEATITUDES LEAD YOU TO JOY

What does the word "blessed" mean? Why does each of the Beatitudes begin with this word? The original term does not imply a person with a full belly or someone who is doing well for themselves, but someone who experiences grace, who follows the path of God, in his grace. Patience, poverty, service to others, consolation: people who understand and share these things are happy and shall be blessed.

In order to give himself to us, God often chooses unthinkable paths. He might choose the path of human limitation, tears or defeat. This is the joy of Easter: Jesus has experienced the stigmata but is alive; he has been through death and has experienced the power of God. The Beatitudes always lead to joy. They are the paths that lead us to joy.

Spiritual Chant IX
He lives! He's risen from the dead!
To every man I shout;
His presence over us is spread,
Goes with us in and out.

To each I say it; each apace
His comrades telleth too—
That straight will dawn in every place
The heavenly kingdom new ...

Weeping no longer shall endure
For him who shuts his eyes;
For, soon or late, a meeting sure
Shall make the loss a prize...

He lives—will sit down by our hearths,
Though all besides had ceased;
Therefore this day shall be the earth's
Rejuvenescence-feast.

Novalis[1]

THE PATH OF LOVE

It is always rewarding for us to read and reflect on the Beatitudes! Jesus proclaimed them in his first great sermon, on the shore of the Sea of Galilee. There was a very large crowd, so Jesus went up on the mountain to teach his disciples. That is why it is known as the Sermon on the Mount.

In the Bible, this mountain is regarded as a place where God appears to Jesus, who proves to be a divine teacher, a new Moses. What does Jesus tell us? He shows us how to live, the way that he himself has taken. Jesus himself *is* the way. He proposes this way as *the path to true happiness*. Throughout his life, from his birth in the stable in Bethlehem until his death on the cross and his resurrection, Jesus embodies the Beatitudes. All the promises of God's kingdom are fulfilled in him.

In proclaiming the Beatitudes, Jesus asks us to follow him and to travel with him along the path of love, the only path that leads to eternal life. It is not an easy journey, and yet the Lord promises us his grace and never abandons us. We face so many challenges in life: poverty, distress, humiliation, the struggle for justice, persecutions, the difficulty of daily conversion, the effort to remain faithful to our call to holiness and many others. But if we open the door to Jesus and allow him to be part of our lives, if we share our joys and sorrows with him, then we will experience the peace and joy that only God, who is infinite love, can give.

THE REPLY OF GOD TO OUR DESIRE FOR HAPPINESS

The Beatitudes are the path that God offers by way of reply to humanity's innate desire for happiness; they complete and perfect the Commandments of the Old Covenant. We are accustomed to learning the Ten Commandments but we are not used to repeating the Beatitudes. Let us try to impress them on our hearts.

Blessed are the poor in spirit,
    for theirs is the kingdom of heaven.
Blessed are those who mourn,
    for they will be comforted.
Blessed are the meek,
    for they will inherit the earth.
Blessed are those who hunger and thirst for
        righteousness,
    for they will be filled.
Blessed are the merciful,
    for they will be shown mercy.
Blessed are the pure in heart,
    for they will see God.

Blessed are the peacemakers,
    for they will be called children of God.
Blessed are those who are persecuted because
      of righteousness,
    for theirs is the kingdom of heaven.
Blessed are you when people insult you, persecute you
    and falsely say all kinds of evil against you because
    of me. Rejoice and be glad, because great is your
    reward in heaven, for in the same way they perse-
    cuted the prophets who were before you.

(Matt. 5:3–12)

These words hold all the newness that Christ brought; all the newness of Christ exists in these words. In fact, the Beatitudes are a portrait of Jesus, his way of life. They are the path to true happiness, which we can travel with the grace that Jesus gives us.

BEATIFIC MEANS HAPPY

What does it mean to be "blessed" (*makarioi* in Greek)? To be blessed means to be happy. Tell me: do you truly want to be happy? In an age when we are constantly being enticed by vain and empty illusions of happiness, we risk settling for less, and thinking small when it comes to the meaning of life. Instead, think big! Open your heart!

A REVOLUTIONARY NOVELTY

The Beatitudes of Jesus are new and revolutionary. They present a model of happiness that runs counter to what is usually communicated by the media and by prevailing wisdom. A mundane way of thinking finds it scandalous that God became one of us and died on a cross! According to the logic of this world of ours, the people Jesus proclaimed as blessed are useless, "losers." Instead, what gets glorified in our world is success at all costs, well-being, the arrogance of power and self-affirmation at the expense of others.

Jesus challenges us to accept his way of life and to choose the right path, the one that will lead to true joy. This is the great challenge of faith. Jesus was not afraid to ask his disciples if they truly wanted to follow him or if they would prefer to take another path (see John 6:67).

Simon Peter had the courage to reply, "Lord, to whom shall we go? You have the words of eternal life" (John 6:68).

If you can say "yes" to Jesus, your life will become meaningful and fruitful.

LET'S BREAK DOWN THE PARADOX OF THE BEATITUDES

Jesus says two things of his people: that they are blessed and that they are poor; indeed, that they are blessed because they are poor.

How does this work? It works because Jesus' disciples do not find joy in money, power or other material goods; they find joy in the gifts they receive every day from God: life, creation, brothers and sisters and so on. These are the gifts of life.

His followers are content to share the goods they possess because they live according to the logic of God. And what is the logic of God? Gratuitousness. The disciples have learned to live with gratuitousness. Poverty is an attitude toward the meaning of life: Jesus' disciples do not think they already know everything, but rather, they know that every day they must learn something. This is poverty: the awareness of having to learn every day. Because of this attitude, Jesus' disciples are humble, open people, unprejudiced and flexible in their thinking.

In other words, the disciple accepts *the paradox of the Beatitudes*, which declares that those who are poor, who lack many things and know it, are blessed, or happy. Humanly speaking, we are inclined to think differently: happy are those who are rich, with many goods; happy are those who receive applause and are the envy of many; happy are those who experience certainty. But this is a worldly mindset; it is not the way of thinking of the Beatitudes! Jesus, on the contrary, declares worldly success to be a failure, since it is based on a kind of selfishness that swells the heart and then leaves it empty. Faced with the paradox of the Beatitudes, disciples allow themselves to be challenged, aware that it is not God who must enter into our mindset, but we into his.

This requires a journey that may sometimes be wearisome but is always accompanied by joy because the disciple of Jesus feels the joy that comes from Jesus. Let us remember that the first word Jesus says is, "Blessed." From this comes the name of the Beatitudes. "Blessed" is a synonym for being a disciple of Jesus. By freeing us from the bondage of self-centeredness, the Lord breaks down our limitations, dissolves our hardness and opens up to us true happiness, which is often found where we do not expect it to be. It is he who guides our life, not we ourselves with our preconceptions and demands. Disciples, in the end, are those who let themselves be led by Jesus, who open their hearts to Jesus, who listen to him and follow his path.

We might then ask ourselves: do I have the willingness and flexibility of the disciples? Or do I behave rigidly, like someone who thinks they are in the right, someone who thinks they are decent, who feels they have already arrived? Do I allow myself to be broken down by the paradox of the Beatitudes, or do I stay within the comfortable confines of my own ideas? And finally, in keeping with the logic of the Beatitudes and setting aside all hardships and difficulties, do I feel the joy inherent in following Jesus? This is the decisive trait of a disciple: if they feel joy in their hearts. Let us not forget this joy in our hearts. This is the touchstone for knowing if a person is a disciple: does he or she have joy in their heart? Do I have joy in my heart?

A THORN IN THE SIDE OF THE WORLD

The poor in spirit, the meek, those who thirst for holiness and mercy, the pure in heart, mourners and peacemakers may all be subjected to persecution because of Christ. Ultimately, however, this persecution is a cause for joy and a great reward in heaven. The way of the Beatitudes is a path related to Easter which leads us from a worldly life to a holy one, from a life led by the flesh, which is to say selfishness, to one guided by the Spirit.

The world, with all its idols, compromises and priorities, has a difficult time accepting this kind of spiritual life. The "structures of sin" that are produced by the human mind and lie outside the Spirit of truth do not want to have anything to do with poverty, meekness and purity. They see living life according to the Gospel as a mistake and a problem, something to isolate. "These people are idealists or fanatics," they tend to say.

In a world that revolves around money, anyone who shows that life can be lived through giving and sacrifice becomes a nuisance to the system of greed. The word "nuisance" here is key; bearing witness as a Christian, which is so good for the many people who experience it, bothers people with a worldly mindset. They see it as a form of chastisement. Something about the holy beauty present in the life of the children of God is unsettling to them. It demands that people take a stance: either allow your existence to be called into question and open up to goodness, or reject that light and harden your heart.

MEEK AND HUMBLE OF HEART

"Blessed are the meek, for they will inherit the earth" (Matt. 5:5). Meekness, brothers and sisters! Meekness and gentleness are qualities of Jesus, who said of himself, "Learn from me, for I am gentle and humble in heart" (Matt. 11:29).

The meek are those who know how to control themselves, who make room for others, who listen to these others and respect their ways of living, their needs and their requests. They do not intend to overwhelm or diminish others; they do not want to tower over or dominate everything, nor do they want to impose their ideas or interests to the detriment of others. These people, who are unappreciated by a worldly mentality, are precious in the eyes of God, who grants them the promised land, which is to say, eternal life. This Beatitude, too, begins here on earth and concludes in heaven, in Christ.

In this era of great aggression, both in the world and in our daily lives, when the first thing that comes out of us is aggression or defensiveness, we need meekness to move forward on the path of holiness. We must always listen and respect, but not attack: this is meekness.

HAPPY ARE THE POOR

"Blessed are the poor in spirit, for theirs is the kingdom of heaven" (Matt. 5:3). We might wonder how a person who is poor of heart can be happy, when their only treasure is the kingdom of heaven. But therein lies the reason: a person with a free heart, one who is unimpeded by so many worldly things, is "awaited" in the kingdom of heaven.

THE LOGIC OF LOVE

Jesus proclaims that the poor, the hungry, the suffering and the persecuted are *blessed*. He *admonishes* those who are rich, who are complacent, who laugh at others and are praised by the people. The reason behind this paradoxical Beatitude lies in the fact that God is close to those who suffer; he intercedes to free them from their bondage. Jesus sees this; he sees the Beatitude beyond its negative reality. And likewise, his "woe to you" attitude directed at those who are financially well off (see Luke 6:24–6) helps wake them up from the dangerous deceit of egotism and opens them up to the logic of love.

A COMPASSIONATE HEART

"Blessed are the merciful, for they will be shown mercy" (Matt. 5:7). Blessed are those who know how to forgive, who show heartfelt compassion, who are capable of offering the very best to others—the best! Not what is left over, but the best!

HAPPY ARE THOSE WHO KNOW HOW TO FORGIVE

Happy are those who know how to forgive, who have mercy on others, who do not judge everything and everyone, but try to put themselves in other people's shoes.

We all need forgiveness—all of us. This is why, at the beginning of Mass, we recognize ourselves for what we are: sinners. It isn't an expression or a formality: it is an act of truth. "Lord, have mercy on me." If we are capable of giving others the forgiveness we ask for, we are blessed. As we say in the Lord's Prayer, "Forgive us our trespasses as we forgive those who trespass against us."

The Canticle of the Creatures
Most High, all-powerful, good Lord,
Yours are the praises, the glory, and the honor,
    and all blessing.

To You alone, Most High, do they belong,
and no human is worthy to mention Your name.

Praised be You, my Lord, with all Your creatures,
especially Sir Brother Sun,
Who is the day and through whom You give us light.

And he is beautiful and radiant with great splendor;
and bears a likeness of You, Most High One.

Praised be You, my Lord, through Sister Moon
and the stars,
in heaven You formed them clear and precious
and beautiful.

Praised be You, my Lord, through Brother Wind,
and through the air, cloudy and serene, and every
kind of weather,
through whom You give sustenance to Your
creatures.

Praised be You, my Lord, through Sister Water,
who is very useful and humble and precious and
chaste.

Praised be You, my Lord, through Brother Fire,
through whom You light the night,
and he is beautiful and playful and robust and
strong.

Praised be You, my Lord, through our Sister
Mother Earth,
who sustains and governs us,
and who produces various fruit with colored flowers and herbs.

Praised be You, my Lord, through those who give
     pardon for Your
love, and bear infirmity and tribulation.

Blessed are those who endure in peace
for by You, Most High, shall they be crowned.

Praised be You, my Lord, through our Sister
     Bodily Death,
from whom no one living can escape.

Woe to those who die in mortal sin.
Blessed are those whom death will find in Your
     most holy will,
for the second death shall do them no harm.

Praise and bless my Lord and give Him thanks
and serve Him with great humility.

St. Francis of Assisi[2]

WE ARE BORN SO AS TO NEVER DIE

It is not a matter of doing extraordinary things, but of following, each and every day, the way that leads us to heaven, to family, back home. Today we catch a glimpse of our future and celebrate what we were born for: we were born so as to never die. We were born to enjoy God's happiness! The Lord encourages us and says to those setting out on the path of the Beatitudes: "Rejoice and be glad, because great is your reward in heaven" (Matt. 5:12).

PART 7

HAPPINESS IS CONCRETE LOVE

THE LOVE OF GOD THAT EMBRACES US

The Italian word for mercy, *misericordia*, is composed of two words: misery and heart, *miseria* and *cuore*. The heart indicates the capacity to love; mercy is the love that embraces the misery of the human person. It is a love that "feels" another's poverty as its own, with the goal of freeing them from it.

"This is love: not that we loved God, but that he loved us and sent his Son as an atoning sacrifice for our sins" (1 John 4:10). The Word became flesh and he wanted to share in all our frailties. He wanted to experience the human condition, going as far as taking the cross upon himself to experience all the pain of human existence. Such is the depth of his compassion and mercy: self-abasement in order to stand by wounded humanity. No sin can erase his merciful closeness or prevent him from offering the grace of conversion, as long as we ask for it. Indeed, sin itself makes the love of God even more radiant; in order to free a slave, God sacrificed his Son.

WE ARE ALL DEBTORS

We are all debtors. All of us. We are in debt to God, who is so generous with us and with all our brothers and sisters. Everyone knows that they are not the father or mother that they should be, the bride or groom, the brother or sister. We are all in debt in some way in life. And we need mercy. We know that we have done wrong. There is always something lacking in the good that we should have done.

But our poverty becomes a strength that leads us to forgive! We are debtors, and if we shall be measured with the same measure with which we measure others, then it would suit us to be expansive and forgive debts; we should forgive (see Luke 6:38). Everyone should remember that they need to forgive, that they are in need of forgiveness and that they need patience. This is the secret to mercy: by forgiving, one is forgiven. In this, God precedes us and forgives us first (see Rom. 5:8). In receiving his forgiveness, we become capable of forgiving. One's own misery and lack of justice become opportunities to open oneself up to the kingdom of heaven, to expand, to make room for God, who is mercy.

[Francis] would remember him always, he thought, the good old man with his worn face and kindly eyes and shabby soutane; there was in him, surely, the fabric of a saint. When he was not addressing the community he seemed to spend all his time on his knees, at all hours of the day and night, in the chapel, Francis had observed. He had seen him there once at midnight when he had come in from walking beside the lake in what was for him the insomniac moonlight; he had gone into the chapel to pray before going to bed and seen the old man kneeling there, his eyes closed, the crucifix in his clasped hands, tears rolling down his face... The incident made a profound impression on him. In his room he took his own crucifix from above his bed and knelt a long time on the bare boards with it in his hands; he did not pray, and yet his whole being prayed in a passionate penitence; it was as though he were involved in a tremendous act of contrition. Blessed Saint Augustine, his heart prayed, help me, for I too have come late to the ancient and eternal beauty that is truth. Help me, O my God, for late I have loved Thee...

Ethel Mannin[1]

THE ONLY PATH TO OVERCOME EVIL

I meet many young people who say that they are tired of how divided the world is, with its endless clashes between factions; its wars, with religion being used as justification for violence. We must ask the Lord to give us the grace to be merciful to those who do us wrong, just as Jesus on the cross prayed for those who crucified him by saying, "Father, forgive them, for they do not know what they are doing" (Luke 23:34).

Mercy is the only way to overcome evil. Justice is, of course, necessary, but on its own it is not enough. Justice and mercy must walk in unity.

THE RECIPROCITY OF FORGIVENESS

The fifth Beatitude says, "Blessed are the merciful, for they will be shown mercy" (Matt. 5:7). This Beatitude is unique: it is the only one in which the cause and the fruit of happiness coincide: mercy. Those who show mercy will find mercy.

The reciprocity of forgiveness is not only found here in this Beatitude; it also appears throughout the Gospel. How could it be otherwise? Mercy is the very heart of God! Jesus says, "Do not judge, and you will not be judged. Do not condemn, and you will not be condemned. Forgive, and you will be forgiven" (Luke 6:37). It is reciprocal.

In the Lord's Prayer, we pray, "And forgive us our debts, as we also have forgiven our debtors" (Matt. 6:12). This request returns at the end of the prayer: "For if you forgive other people when they sin against you, your heavenly Father will also forgive you. But if you do not forgive others their sins, your Father will not forgive your sins" (Matt. 6:14–15).

These are two things that cannot be divided: forgiveness granted and forgiveness received. However, many people struggle with this: they cannot forgive. Often the harm they have received is so great that being able to forgive feels like climbing a very high mountain. It requires enormous effort. A person might think, no, it cannot be done. The reciprocity of mercy shows that we have to rethink our perspective. But we cannot do this alone; we need the grace of God—we must ask for it. Indeed, if the fifth Beatitude promises mercy, and if in the Lord's Prayer we ask for the forgiveness of sins, it means that we are essentially sinners and we need to find mercy!

WHAT DOES IT MEAN
TO BE MERCIFUL?

I always like to link the Beatitudes with Matthew 25, where Jesus presents us with works of mercy and tells us that our judgment depends on them. For this reason I ask you to go back to the corporal works of mercy: feed the hungry, give drink to the thirsty, clothe the naked, welcome foreigners, assist the sick, visit the imprisoned and bury the dead.

And let us not overlook the spiritual works of mercy: offer counsel to those in doubt, teach the ignorant, admonish sinners, comfort the sorrowful, forgive offenses, be patient with troublesome people, and pray to God for both the living and the dead. Mercy does not just imply being a "good person," nor is it mere sentimentality. There are practical ways for us to prove that we are truly disciples of Jesus, ways that we can show our credibility as Christians in today's world.

WE NEED FORGIVENESS
LIKE WE NEED AIR

Where does our mercy come from? Jesus told us, "Be merciful, just as your Father is merciful" (Luke 6:36). The more one welcomes in the Father's love, the more we can love.

Mercy is not one aspect of life among many others; it is the center of the Christian life. There is no Christianity without mercy. If our Christianity does not lead us to mercy, then we have taken a wrong turn somewhere, because mercy is the only true destination of all spiritual journeys. It is one of the most beautiful fruits of charity.

God's mercy is our liberation and our happiness. We live

thanks to mercy and we cannot afford to go without: it is the air we breathe. We are too poor to set conditions. We need to forgive because we need to be forgiven.

A CONCRETE LOVE

God's mercy is very real, and we are all called on to experience it first-hand.

When I was seventeen years old, before going out with friends, I decided to go into a church. I met a priest there who inspired great confidence in me and I felt the desire to open my heart in Confession. That meeting changed my life! I discovered that when we open our hearts with humility and transparency, we contemplate God's mercy in a very concrete way.

I felt certain that God was waiting for me through that priest, even before I walked into his church. We look and look for him, but he always precedes us. He is always looking for us and he always finds us first.

Maybe you have something that weighs heavily on your heart. You might think to yourself, "I did this, I did that..." Do not be afraid! God is waiting for you! God is the Father: he is always waiting for you! How wonderful it is to feel the merciful embrace of the Father in the sacrament of reconciliation, to discover that the confessional is a place of mercy, and to allow ourselves to be moved by the merciful love of the Lord who always forgives us!

GOD'S LOVE IS VISCERAL

God's mercy is not an abstract idea, but a concrete reality through which he shows his love, the way a father or mother is moved to their very depths out of love for their child. God's mercy is truly a visceral kind of love. It gushes forth from our depths naturally, full of tenderness and compassion, indulgence and mercy.

EACH OF US IS A PRODIGAL SON

In Luke 15, we find the three parables of mercy: the lost sheep, the lost coin and the prodigal son. In these three parables we are struck by God's joy, the joy that God feels when he finds and forgives a sinner. Yes, God's joy is forgiveness! This sums up the entire Gospel.

Each of us is that lost little lamb, the coin that was mislaid, the son who squandered his freedom on false idols and illusions of happiness, who lost everything. But God does not forget us; the Father never abandons us. He is a patient Father; he always waits for us! He respects our freedom, but he is always faithful. And when we come back to him, he welcomes us like children into his house, for he never ceases, not for one instant, to wait for us with love. And his heart rejoices for every child who returns. He rejoices because he is joy. God feels joy when one of us sinners goes to him and asks his forgiveness.

MERCY HAS A YOUTHFUL FACE

Mercy always has a youthful face. A merciful heart is motivated to leave comforts behind, to move out of its comfort zone, to go forth and encounter others, to embrace everyone. A merciful heart is able to offer refuge to those who never had or have lost their homes; it knows how to build a home and a family for those who have been forced to emigrate; it knows the meaning of tenderness and compassion. A merciful heart knows how to share its bread with the hungry and welcome refugees and migrants. The word "mercy" is equivalent to saying opportunity, future, commitment, trust, openness, hospitality, compassion and dreams.

When the heart is open and capable of dreaming, there is room for mercy; there is room to embrace those who are suffering; there is room for standing beside those who do not have peace in their hearts or the bare necessities to get by, or who lack the most beautiful thing of all: faith. Show mercy.

LET US REMEMBER OUR SINS, NOT OUR SUCCESSES

All the times we have sinned, all the times we have experienced our limitations and shortcomings and failures, all the times we have fallen, Jesus has always seen us. He drew close to us, extended his hand to us and showed us mercy. To whom? To you, to me, to everyone. All of us can think back and remember the many times that the Lord looked upon us, drew close to us and showed us mercy. All the times that the Lord kept trusting us, he kept betting on us (see Ezek. 16).

It does us such good to return to this truth, to remember how the Lord continued to bring mercy to our lives, placing the memory of our sin and not our presumed successes at the center, so that we could grow with humble awareness and not merely distance ourselves from our lives—ours, not those of others, not the person next to us, and definitely not that of our people—so that we could go back to being awed by God's mercy. This is a certain message and sound teaching; these are not empty words.

Spiritual Chant V
If I him but have,
If he be but mine,
If my heart, hence to the grave,
Ne'er forgets his love divine—
Know I nought of sadness,
Feel I nought but worship, love, and gladness...

If I him but have,
Glad to sleep I sink;
From his heart the flood he gave
Shall to me be food and drink
And—oh, soft compelling!—
All shall mollify with deep indwelling.

Novalis[2]

LOVE IS NOT AN ABSTRACT WORD

Mercy is a key word that indicates God's action toward us. He does not limit himself merely to affirming his love, but makes it visible and tangible. Love, after all, is never just an abstraction. By its very nature, it indicates something concrete: intentions, attitudes and daily behaviors.

The mercy of God is his loving concern for each one of us. He feels responsible, which is to say that he desires our well-being and wants to see us happy, full of joy and peace. The merciful love of Christians must exist on the same wavelength. Just as the Father loves, so do his children. Just as he is merciful, so we are called to be merciful to each other.

CHARITY IS A GIFT

Charity is a gift that brings meaning to our lives. It enables us to view those in need as members of our own family, friends, brothers or sisters. Even a small amount, if given with love, can grow into a resource of life and happiness. Such was the case with the jar of flour and jug of oil belonging to the widow of Zarephath, who offered bread to the prophet Elijah (see 1 Kings 17:7–16). Such was also the case with the loaves that were blessed, broken and given by Jesus to the disciples to distribute to the crowd (see Mark 6:30–44). Such is the case too with our almsgiving, whether small or large, when offered with joy and simplicity.

LIVING CHARITY

Only God forgives sins, but he asks that we be ready to forgive others as he forgives us: "And forgive us our debts, as we also have forgiven our debtors" (Matt. 6:12). How sad it is when our hearts are closed and we are unable to forgive! Resentment, anger and revenge gain the upper hand, making our lives miserable and blocking a joyful commitment to mercy.

THE LAST WORD HAS
NOT BEEN SPOKEN

Far from being an idea, a desire or a theory—much less an ideology—mercy is a concrete way of "coming into contact" with weakness, of bonding with others, of drawing closer to others. It is a concrete way of encountering people when they are going through a bad period. It is a way of behaving that allows us to give the best of ourselves so that others can feel as though, in their lives, the last word has not yet been spoken, so that people who have felt crushed by the burden of their sins feel some relief at being given another chance. Far from being just a beautiful word, mercy is the concrete act by which God seeks to connect with his children.

DO NOT FEAR ANY EVIL

Each one of us has our own life story. Each one of us has our sins. And if we do not remember them immediately, think for a minute: you will remember them. And then thank God when you find them, because if you do not, you are corrupt.

Each one of us has his or her own sins. Let us look to the Lord, who performs justice but who is also extremely merciful. Let us not be ashamed to be part of the Church; let us not be ashamed of being sinners. The Church is Mother to all. Let us thank God that we are not corrupt and recognize that we are, indeed, sinners. May each one of us, seeing how Jesus acted in these cases, entrust ourselves to God's mercy and pray for forgiveness.

> He guides me along the right paths
>   for his name's sake.
> Even though I walk
>   through the darkest valley,
> I will fear no evil,
>   for you are with me;
> your rod and your staff,
>   they comfort me.
>
> (Ps. 23:3–4)

EXPERIENCING THE LIFE OF OTHERS

"Blessed are those who mourn, for they will be comforted" (Matt. 5:4). How can those who weep be happy? And yet those who have never felt sadness, despair or sorrow will never know the power of comfort. Instead, happy are those who can feel moved, who can feel in their hearts the sorrow that exists in their lives and in the lives of others. They will be happy! Because the tender hand of God the Father will comfort them and will caress them.

THE PATH THAT GOES FROM THE HEART TO THE HANDS

We need to understand and accept what God does for us: God does not think, love or act out of fear, but because he trusts us and expects us to change. This needs to be our mode of operation: "Go and do likewise" (Luke 10:37). Our way of treating others should never be based on fear, but on God's hope in our ability to change.

Actions done out of fear separate, divide, surgically disconnect one from the other, and build walls and a false sense of security. Instead, actions done with the hope for change and conversion encourage, incite, look to the future, create space for opportunity and keep us moving forward. Actions done out of fear hint at guilt, punishment, an attitude of, "You were wrong." Actions filled with hope for transformation place an emphasis on trust, learning, getting to one's feet, always trying to generate new opportunities.

How many times? Seventy times seven (see Matt. 18:22). For this reason, treating people with mercy awakens creativity.

It places an emphasis on the face of the person, on their life, their history and their daily existence. Merciful actions do not happen by following a model or a recipe; they are filled with the healthy spirit of freedom. They seek out what would be best for the other in a way that is meaningful. This activates and engages all our abilities and gifts and has us step outside our closed circles. Actions based on hope for change are filled with a kind of restless intelligence that makes our hearts beat fast and readies our hands for action. It is a journey that goes from the heart to the hands.

AN EXERCISE IN MERCY

If we live according to the law of "Eye for eye, and tooth for tooth," we will never get out of the spiral of evil (see Matt. 5:38–42). The evil one is clever and deludes us into thinking that with our human justice we can save ourselves and the world. In reality, only the justice of God can save us! And the justice of God is revealed in the cross: the cross is the judgment of God on all of us and on this world.

But how does God judge us? By giving his life for us! This is the supreme act of justice that defeated the prince of the world once and for all, and this supreme act of justice is the supreme act of mercy. Jesus calls on all of us to follow this path: "Be merciful, just as your Father is merciful" (Luke 6:36).

I ask of you one thing. Think of someone who you are annoyed with, someone who has made you angry or someone you do not like. Let us think of that person and pray for them in silence. Let us show mercy to this person.

SPIRITUAL ALZHEIMER'S

We know that spiritual Alzheimer's has set in when we forget how the Lord has treated us, when we start to feel shock and surprise and when we begin to judge and divide up society. We take on a separatist mindset that, without us realizing it, leads us to fragment our social and communal reality even more. We break up the present by creating groups: good and bad, saints and sinners. Our memory loss leads us to forget the richest reality we possess and the clearest teaching we have received.

Although we are all sinners, the Lord never stops treating us with mercy. The apostle Paul never forgot that he was once on the other side, that he was chosen last. Mercy is not a theory to be brandished so that we sound noble and righteous, but a history of sins to be remembered. Whose sins? Ours: mine and yours. Mercy is also a show of love to be praised. Whose love? The love of God, who has shown me mercy.

A NEED FOR CONSOLATION

Another face of mercy is *consolation*. "Comfort, comfort my people" (Isa. 40:1) is the heartfelt plea that the prophet continues to make today, so that a word of hope may reach all those who experience suffering and pain. Let us never allow ourselves to be robbed of the hope born from faith in the risen Lord.

While it is true that we are often sorely tested, we must never lose our certainty of the Lord's love for us. His mercy finds expression in the closeness, affection and support that many of our brothers and sisters can offer us in times of sadness and affliction. The drying of tears is one way to break the vicious cycle of solitude in which we often find ourselves trapped.

We all need consolation; no one is spared suffering, pain and misunderstanding. How much pain can be caused by a spiteful remark born of envy, jealousy or anger! What great suffering is caused by the experience of betrayal, violence and abandonment! How much sorrow we experience when faced with the death of a loved one! And yet God is never far from us in such moments of sadness and trouble. A reassuring word, an empathetic embrace, a gentle caress, a prayer: all can relay love and makes us stronger. All these things express God's closeness through consolation and can be offered by our brothers and sisters.

I call it consolation when some interior movement in the soul is caused, through which the soul comes to be inflamed with love of its Creator and Lord; and when it can in consequence love no created thing on the face of the earth in itself, but in the Creator of them all.

Likewise, when it sheds tears that move to love of its Lord, whether out of sorrow for one's sins, or for the Passion of Christ our Lord, or because of other things directly connected with His service and praise.

Finally, I call consolation every increase of hope, faith and charity, and all interior joy which calls and attracts to heavenly things and to the salvation of one's soul, quieting it and giving it peace in its Creator and Lord.

St. Ignatius of Loyola[3]

MERCY CAN BE LEARNED

Mercy is learned from experience. It is learned from sensing that God continues to trust in us and calls us to be his missionaries, that he constantly sends us forth to treat our brothers and sisters in the same way that he has treated us. Mercy is learned because our Father continues to forgive us. There is already too much suffering in people's lives; they do not need us to add more to it. Learning to show mercy means learning from the Master how to be neighborly without being afraid of the outcast or those who are "tainted" and marked by sin; to learn to hold out our hand to those who have fallen, without being afraid of what people will say. Any behavior that lacks mercy, however right it might seem, ends up becoming mistreatment. Our challenge is to empower paths of hope, to encourage paths that treat people well so that mercy may shine forth.

SILENCE IS PARTICIPATORY

Sometimes silence can be helpful, especially when we cannot find words to reply to the questions raised by people who suffer. We can make up for our lack of words by showing compassion, by showing love, by reaching out a hand. It is not true that silence is an act of surrender. On the contrary, it is a moment of strength and love. Silence is part of the language of consolation because it is a concrete way of sharing in the suffering of a brother or sister.

THE TENDERNESS OF THE LORD

Let us all say, "The Lord is my God and my Savior!" The apostle Paul says, "The Lord is near" (Phil. 4:5). Nothing should perturb us because he is close by. The greatest mercy lies in knowing his presence is in our midst. He walks with us, he shows us the path of love, he lifts us up when we fall (and with such tenderness!), he supports us in our labors, he accompanies us in every circumstance of life. He opens our eyes so we can see our own wretchedness as well as that of the world, but at the same time he fills us with hope.

"The peace of God...will guard your hearts and your minds in Christ Jesus," St. Paul tells us (Phil. 4:7). This is the source of our peaceful and happy life. Nothing and no one can deprive us of this peace and joy, despite all the suffering and trials of life. The Lord gently opens his heart to us, opens us to his love. The Lord is allergic to formality. Let us cultivate this experience of mercy, peace and hope in imitation of him, who gave us everything, so that everything may be given without expecting anything in return. This is his mercy.

LET GO OF RANCOR

Jesus says that mercy is not only an action of the Father, but also necessary for understanding who his true children are. In short, we are called on to show mercy because mercy has been shown to us. Forgiving an offense is the clearest expression of merciful love, and for us Christians it is imperative; it is part of who we are.

How hard it seems at times to forgive! And yet forgiveness is the tool that has been placed in our hands so that we may attain serenity in our hearts. Letting go of anger, bitterness, wrath, violence and revenge are necessary for living joyfully. Let us heed the apostle's exhortation: "Do not let the sun go down while you are still angry" (Eph. 4:26). Let us listen, above all, to the words of Jesus who made mercy an ideal of life and a criterion for the credibility of our faith: "Blessed are the merciful, for they will be shown mercy" (Matt. 5:7).

THE UNSPEAKABLE JOY OF FORGIVENESS

Nothing that a repentant sinner places before God's mercy will be excluded from the embrace of his forgiveness. None of us has the right to impose conditions on mercy: it is always a gratuitous act shown by our heavenly Father, an unconditional and undeserved act of love. We cannot run the risk of getting in the way of the freedom of God's love and how he chooses to enter into the life of every person.

Mercy is a concrete action of love that forgives us and transforms our lives. In this way, the divine mystery of mercy is made manifest. God is merciful (see Exod. 34:6). His mercy lasts forever (see Ps. 136). Generation after generation, he embraces those who trust in him and changes them by giving them his own life.

Mercy gives rise to joy; our hearts open up to the hope of a new life. The joy of forgiveness is unspeakable, but it is evident every time we experience it. The source of this joy lies in the love with which God comes toward us, breaking through the walls of selfishness that surround us, making us, in turn, instruments of mercy.

HUBRIS AND PRIDE FORM A BARRIER

Being Christian does not render us flawless. Like Matthew the tax collector, each of us trusts in the grace of the Lord despite our sins. We are all sinners; we have all sinned. By calling to Matthew, Jesus shows sinners that he does not care about their pasts, their social status or other external conventions, but rather, he offers them a new future.

Once I heard a beautiful saying: "There is no saint without a past and no sinner without a future." This captures what Jesus does. There is no saint without a past and no sinner without a future. It is enough to respond to the call with a humble and sincere heart. The Church is not a community of perfect people, but a group of disciples on a journey, who follow the Lord because they know they are sinners and need his forgiveness. Christian life is a school of humility that opens us up to grace.

Such behavior is not understood by those who have the arrogance to believe they are "just" and better than others. Hubris and pride get in the way of seeing ourselves as in need of salvation; they prevent us from gazing on the merciful face of God and from acting with mercy. They are a wall, a barrier, that gets in the way of our relationship with God. And yet, this is precisely Jesus' mission: he comes looking for all of us to heal our wounds and to call us to follow him in the name of love.

THE FIRST ACT

Love is the first act with which God makes himself known to us and comes toward us. Let us keep our hearts open and trust that God loves us. His love always precedes us, it accompanies us and stays by us, despite our sins.

THE TIME OF MERCY

Now is the time of mercy. Each day of our journey is marked by God's presence. He guides our steps with the power of the grace that the Spirit pours into our hearts to make them capable of loving.

Now is the time of mercy for each one of us and all of us, so that no one thinks they are cut off from God's closeness and the power of his tender love.

Now is the time of mercy so that those who are weak and vulnerable, distant and alone, feel the presence of brothers and sisters who can help them in their need.

Now is the time of mercy so that the poor feel the respect and concern from those who have overcome indifference and discovered what is truly essential in life.

Now is the time of mercy so that no sinner ever tires of asking for forgiveness or feeling the welcoming embrace of the Father.

PART 8

HAPPINESS A HUNDRED TIMES OVER IN THIS LIFE

GOD LOVES US

Allow me to share the most fundamental truth with you: God loves you. It does not matter if you have heard it before or not. I want to remind you of it. God loves you. Never doubt this, whatever may happen to you in life. You are, in all situations, infinitely loved.

GOD REJOICES WITH US

God loves us so much that he rejoices along with us. His love for us is gratuitous, limitless and unconditional.

GOD REJOICES FOR US

His love is not glum; it is pure joy, and we are overcome by it whenever we allow ourselves to be loved by him:

The LORD your God is with you,
    the Mighty Warrior who saves.
He will take great delight in you;
    in his love he will no longer rebuke you,
    but will rejoice over you with singing.

(Zeph. 3:17)

You are truly precious for him; you are not insignificant. You are important to him, for you are the work of his hands. This is why he is concerned for you and looks to you with affection. You must have faith in God's memory. It is not a "hard drive" that saves and archives all our data. His memory is a heart filled with tender compassion, one that finds joy in deleting all traces of evil from us. He does not keep track of your mistakes, although he is always willing to help you learn from them. He does this because he loves you. Try to sit still for a moment, silence the noise within and rest for a second in his loving embrace.

Spiritual Chant XI
Hero of love, oh, take me, take me!
Thou art my life! my world! my gold!
Should the firm earth itself forsake me,
I know who me will scathless hold.

I see thee my lost loves restoring!
True to me evermore thou art.
Low at thy feet heaven sinks adoring,
And yet thou dwellest in my heart!

Novalis[1]

THIRST FOR THE INFINITE

The quest for happiness is common to all people of all times and ages. God placed the irrepressible desire for happiness and fulfillment in the hearts of each and every man and woman.

Have you ever noticed the restlessness of your heart? And how it continuously searches for a treasure that can satisfy its thirst for the infinite?

WELCOME THE GIFT

Jesus wants to be your friend, your brother, a teacher of truth and life, someone who reveals the path to take that will lead you to happiness and to the fulfillment of yourself in accordance with God's plan for each of us. Jesus' friendship, which brings us mercy and the love of God, is free; it is an entirely pure gift. He asks nothing of you in exchange, just that you welcome him in. Jesus wants to love you for who you are, with all your weaknesses and frailties, so that, moved by his love, you may be renewed.

LEARN TO READ THE BOOK OF YOUR LIFE STORY

In life, we always have to make decisions, and to make decisions we have to go on a journey: we have to undertake a path of discernment. Every important activity has instructions that need to be followed and learned in order to obtain the desired effect. A vital ingredient for discernment is knowing *one's own life story*. Knowing one's own life story is an essential ingredient, if we want to call it that, for discernment.

Our life is the most precious "book" we have been given. It is a book that, unfortunately, many do not read or, rather, they do so too late, as they approach death. And yet, it is precisely in this book that we find what we pointlessly seek out elsewhere.

St. Augustine, a great seeker of the truth, understood this and reread his life. As he did, he noted the silent and discreet, but clear, steps of the presence of the Lord. At the end of this journey, he noted with wonder, "You were within, and I without, and there I did seek you; I, unlovely, rushed heedlessly among the things of beauty You made. You were with me, but I was not with you."[2] From this comes his invitation to cultivate our inner life so we can find what we are seeking: "Return to yourself. In our interior the truth resides."[3]

I would like to extend this invitation to all of you and even to myself: Return to yourself. Read your life story. Assess how your journey has been. Do it with serenity. Return to yourself.

We often experience the same things that Augustine did. We may have found ourselves imprisoned by thoughts that lead us away from ourselves, by stereotypical messages that harm us. For example, we may think, "I am worthless," and it brings us down. Or we may think, "Nothing ever goes right for me," and this, too, brings us down. Or else, "I will never achieve anything worthwhile," and this brings us down further. All these pessimistic phrases bring us down. Reading our own life story means recognizing the presence of these toxic elements, but it also allows us to broaden our narratives and notice other things that make the story richer and more complex, things that allow us to grasp the delicate ways in which God enters into our lives.

DISTINGUISHING LIGHT
FROM SHADOW

If we want to become better, we must learn to distinguish light from darkness. Where do we begin? You can start by asking yourself: what are the things that first strike me as glittery and seductive, but then leave me with a feeling of deep emptiness? Those are the shadows!

What, on the other hand, is good for me and brings peace to my heart, even if at first it asks me to give up certain conveniences or to master certain instincts? That is the light!

And, I ask myself, what strength enables us to separate the light from the darkness within? What strength enables us to say "no" to the temptations of evil and "yes" to all that is good? Freedom. Freedom does not mean doing everything I want and acting as I please. Freedom is not what I can do despite others, but what I can do for others. Freedom is not a whim; it is responsibility. Freedom, along with life, is the greatest gift that our heavenly Father has given us.

STRUGGLING EVERY DAY WITH
THE DARKNESS WITHIN

Each and every day you are called to bring new light into the world: the light of your eyes, the light of your smile, the light of the goodness that you, and you alone, can bring. No one else. But to come into this light, to be reborn, every day you need to fight off the darkness. That's right: every single day there is a clash between light and darkness. It does not take place somewhere "out there"; it happens within each of us. It takes courage. It takes strong, heartfelt decisions to resist the darkness of lies and to follow the way of light.

"Ah!" said Gandalf. "That is a very long story. The beginnings lie back in the Black Years, which only the lore-masters now remember. If I were to tell you all that tale, we should still be sitting here when Spring had passed into Winter.

"But last night I told you of Sauron the Great, the Dark Lord. The rumors that you have heard are true: he has indeed arisen again and left his hold in Mirkwood and returned to his ancient fastness in the Dark Tower of Mordor. That name even you hobbits have heard of, like a shadow on the borders of old stories. Always after a defeat and a respite, the Shadow takes another shape and grows again."

"I wish it need not have happened in my time," said Frodo.

"So do I," said Gandalf, "and so do all who live to see such times. But that is not for them to decide. All we have to decide is what to do with the time that is given us."

J. R. R. Tolkien[4]

DEFEND TRUE BEAUTY

Allow your beauty to shine! Not the fashionable beauty of worldly things, but true beauty. May you bring to our world, rife with unpleasantness, the beauty that has always belonged to us, from the first moment of creation, when God made humankind in his own image and saw that it was very good. This beauty must be both shared and defended. For if it is true that beauty will save the world, as Prince Myshkin said in Dostoevsky's *The Idiot*,[5] then we must be careful that the world protects and saves beauty. To achieve this, I invite young people to embrace the Global Compact on Beauty,[6] for education does not exist without beauty.

The beauty in question here is not the kind that pertains to Narcissus, who fell in love with his own reflection and drowned in the lake in which he saw himself mirrored. Nor is it the kind of beauty that creates a pact with evil, like Dorian Gray, who found himself with a disfigured face when the spell ended. No, the beauty in question here never fades because it is a reflection of divine beauty. Indeed, our God is simultaneously good, true and beautiful. Beauty is one of the privileged ways of finding him.

TAKING CARE OF OUR HEARTS AND RELATIONSHIPS

The Gospels speak of how Jesus dismantled the prevailing concepts of ritual purity and the rules that forbade coming into contact with things and people (including lepers and strangers) who were considered impure. To the Pharisees, who, like so many Jews of their time, ate nothing without first performing ritual ablutions and observing many traditions associated with cleansing dishes, Jesus categorically said, "Nothing outside a person can defile them by going into them...For it is from within, out of a person's heart, that evil thoughts come—sexual immorality, theft, murder, adultery, greed, malice, deceit, lewdness, envy, slander, arrogance and folly" (Mark 7:15, 21–2).

So what kind of happiness comes from a pure heart? The list of evils that Jesus mentions share a common element: interpersonal relationships. Each of us has to learn to discern what can "defile" our heart, and what can shape our conscience in a right and sensible manner so that we can "test and approve what God's will is—his good, perfect and pleasing will" (Rom. 12:2).

Of course, we need to show a healthy concern for creation, for the purity of our air, water and food, but even more we need to protect the purity of what is most precious to us: *our hearts and our relationships*. This "human ecology" will help us breathe the pure air that comes from beauty, true love and holiness.

THE SOURCE OF OUR JOY

The more we love, the more we know how to give. This is another key that helps us understand life. It is wonderful to meet people who love generously and who lovingly share their lives with others. We can say about them the same things that we say about God: they love so much that they are willing to give up their lives. It is not only what we can make or earn that matters; in the end, it is all the love we are able to give.

This is *the source of joy*! God loved the world so much that he gave up his Son (see John 3:16).

Sometimes we look for joy where there is none to be found: in illusions that vanish, in dreams of glory, in the apparent security of material possessions, in the cult of our image and so many other things. But life teaches us that true joy comes from realizing that we are loved gratuitously, from knowing that we are not alone, that we have someone who shares our dreams and who, when we experience shipwreck, is there to help us and lead us to a safe harbor.

> Beyond the windows lay silent, dark, hungry Moscow. Its shops were empty, and as for game and vodka, people had even forgotten to think about such things. And so it turned out that only a life similar to the life of those around us, merging with it without a ripple, is genuine life, and that an unshared happiness is not happiness, so that duck and vodka, when they seem to be the only ones in town, are not even duck and vodka.
>
> Boris Pasternak[7]

DON'T BE A "SLEEPING BEAUTY"

The beauty that Jesus reveals to us is a form of splendor that can be communicated through action, it is a physical beauty that can be shared, it is a courageous beauty that is not afraid of getting its hands dirty or of becoming disfigured to uphold the love of which it is made. Therefore, do not be a "sleeping beauty" in the woods: you are called on to act, to do something. True beauty is always fruitful; it pushes us out and gets us moving. Even the act of contemplating God cannot stay at a standstill; we see this in the story of the three disciples on Mount Tabor at the moment of Jesus' transfiguration: "Lord, it is good for us to be here! If you wish, I will put up three shelters..." (Matt. 17:4). No, now is the time to come down from the mountain and roll up your sleeves.

I wish, for each and every one of you, a *healthy restlessness* in your desires and projects, a restlessness that pushes you to keep walking, to never have the feeling that you have "arrived." Do not cut yourself off from the world by closing yourself off in your room—like a Peter Pan who does not want to grow up, or like a young *hikikomori* who is afraid to face the world—but always be open and courageous.

HAPPY IS THE PERSON WHO SEES GOODNESS IN OTHERS

In the Bible, the devil is called the "father of lies" (John 8:44). He promises, or rather, he would have you believe, that if you do certain things, you will be happy. Afterward, you realize that you are not happy at all, that you followed something that, far from bringing you happiness, made you feel emptier and sadder.

Friends, the devil is a con artist. He makes promise after promise, but never delivers. He never does anything he says. He doesn't make good on his promises. He makes you want things that he can't provide, whether you obtain them or not. He makes you put your hopes in things that will never make you happy. That's his game, his strategy. He talks a lot, offers a lot, but doesn't deliver. He is a con artist because everything he promises us is divisive, leading us to compare ourselves with others, making us step over them to get what we want. He is a con artist because he tells us that we must abandon our friends and not stand by anyone. Everything is based on appearances.

He makes you think that your worth depends on how much you possess.

Then we have Jesus, who asks us to play on his team. He doesn't con us, nor does he promise us the world. He doesn't tell us that we will find happiness in wealth, power and pride. Just the opposite. He shows us a different way. This coach tells his players: happy are the poor in spirit, those who mourn, the meek, those who hunger and thirst for righteousness, the merciful, the pure in heart, those who work for peace, those who are persecuted for righteousness' sake (see Matt. 5:3–12). And he concludes by telling his players to rejoice on account of all this.

Why should we rejoice? Because Jesus doesn't lie to us. He shows us a path that is life and truth. He is the proof of it. This is his style, his way of life, how he provides friendship; this is his relationship with his Father. And he offers it all to us. He would like us to feel like sons and daughters, too, like beloved children.

He does not trick us. He knows that happiness, true happiness, the happiness that can fill our hearts, is not found in designer clothing or expensive brand-name shoes. He knows that real happiness can be found in drawing near to others, in learning how to weep with those who weep, in standing alongside those who are feeling low or in trouble, giving them a shoulder to cry on or a hug. If we don't know how to weep, we don't know how to laugh either, and therefore we don't know how to live.

Jesus knows that true happiness in this world, a world filled with competition, envy and aggression, comes from learning to be patient, from respecting others, from refusing to condemn or judge others. As the saying goes, "When you get angry, you lose." Don't let your heart give in to anger and resentment. Happy are the merciful. Happy are those who know how to put themselves in someone else's shoes, who are able to embrace and forgive.

We have all experienced forgiveness. And how beautiful it is! It is like getting our life back, a new chance. Nothing is more beautiful than being able to start afresh. Life can start all over again.

Happy, too, are those who bring new life and new opportunities. Happy are those who work and sacrifice to do this. All of us have made mistakes, thousands of them. Happy, then, are those who can help others when they make mistakes, when they experience misunderstandings. They are true friends; they do not give up on anyone. They are the pure in heart; they can look beyond the little things and overcome difficulties. Happy, above all, are those who can see the good in other people.

THE GOODNESS THAT IS LACKING

Another "ingredient" that is vital to being able to discern is *desire*. In fact, discernment is a form of searching; searching always stems from something we lack but which we somehow know or intuit we need.

What kind of knowledge is this? Spiritual teachers refer to it with the term "desire," which, fundamentally, is a kind of longing for fullness that never finds complete fulfillment. It is a clear sign of God's presence in us.

Desire is not a momentary craving. No. The Italian word *desiderio* comes from a very beautiful Latin term: *de-sidus*, which literally means "lacking the star." Desire is a kind of lacking of the star, a lack of a reference point that orients the path of our life. It suggests a suffering, an absence and, at the same time, an urge to reach out toward the good that we are missing. Consequently, desire is like a compass I can use to understand where I am and where I am going. Actually, it is a compass that I can use to see if I am standing still or if I am moving forward. A person who never desires anything is a static person, possibly ill, practically dead.

How do we recognize desire? Let us reflect on this: a sincere desire knows how to touch deeply the chords of our being, which is why it does not get extinguished in the face of difficulties or setbacks. It is like feeling thirsty: if we do not find something to drink, we do not give up. On the contrary, the yearning increasingly occupies our thoughts and actions, until we become willing to make any sacrifice in order to quench it. Obstacles and failures do not stifle desire. No, on the contrary, they make our desire even more vivid.

THE GRACE OF HAVING GREAT DESIRES

Many people suffer because they do not know what they want from their lives; they have probably never gotten in touch with their deepest desires. They might have asked themselves, "What do I want from life?" but the answer has always been, "I don't know." This can lead a person to spend their life trying out all sorts of things but never really getting anywhere, consequently wasting precious opportunities. To the degree that even when certain possibilities arise, although desired in theory, they are never actually implemented; the strong desire to pursue something is lacking.

If the Lord were to ask us today the question that he asked the blind man in Jericho—"What do you want me to do for you?" (Mark 10:51)—what would we say? We could ask him to help us discover his deepest desire, which God himself has placed in our heart: "Lord, show me my desire so that I can be a person with great desires." Perhaps the Lord will give us the strength to make them come true. Allowing the Lord, as in the Gospel, to work miracles for us is an immense grace and it lies at the base of all others. We need to learn to say, "Give us desire and make it grow, Lord."

HAPPINESS YOU PURCHASE DOES NOT LAST

You cannot purchase happiness. Whenever you try to buy happiness, you soon realize that it has vanished...The happiness you buy does not last. The only happiness that lasts is love.

The path of love is simple: love God and love your neighbor, your brother or sister, the person by your side who needs love and so many other things.

"But, Father, how do I know if I love God?"

If you love your neighbor, if you do not harbor hatred in your heart, you love God. This is the certain proof.

HAPPINESS EXISTS IN LOVE

The profession of faith in Jesus Christ does not end with words, but needs to be verified by practical choices and gestures, by a life characterized by God's love. It calls for a great life, a life filled with an abundance of love for our neighbor. Jesus tells us that to follow him, to be his disciples, we must deny ourselves the demands of our own selfish pride and take up our own personal cross. Then he gives everyone a fundamental rule: "For whoever wants to save their life will lose it" (Matt. 16:25).

Often in life, for many reasons, we go astray. We look for happiness only in things, or in people we treat as things. But we find happiness only when love, true love, encounters us, surprises us, changes us. Love changes everything! And love can change all of us, each one of us.

LOVE AND ADVENTURE MAKE OUR LIVES GREAT

To be truly original and revolutionary today we need to rebel against the culture of the ephemeral, go beyond superficial instincts and momentary pleasures and choose to love with every fiber of our being, for the rest of our lives. We were not put here just to get by, but to build something with our lives.

Think of the great stories you might have read in novels or seen in unforgettable films or heard in moving tales. There are always two key ingredients: one is love and the other is adventure, heroism. They always go together. For our life to be great, we need both love and heroism. If we look to the crucified Jesus, we find both: boundless love and the courage of giving up one's life. There are no half-measures.

THE PLANK AND SPECK

Tenderness, kindness, humility, meekness and magnanimity. A Christian life is magnanimous; it is grand.

Be merciful, just as your Father is merciful.

Do not judge, and you will not be judged. Do not condemn, and you will not be condemned. Forgive, and you will be forgiven. Give, and it will be given to you. A good measure, pressed down, shaken together and running over, will be poured into your lap. For with the measure you use, it will be measured to you.

(Luke 6:36–8)

If you have a great deal of love, mercy and generosity, you will be judged on that; if you do not, you will be judged on the amount you have.

But how do we set out? What is the first step to take on this path?

The first step is to accuse oneself before accusing others: "First take the plank out of your eye, and then you will see clearly to remove the speck from your brother's eye" (Luke 6:42). Ask yourself, "Am I doing the right thing? Or am I busy judging others, trying to take the specks out of their eyes and accusing them?"

People who do not know how to accuse themselves first become hypocrites. If one of us does not know how to accuse ourself, we are not Christian; we will not gain access to this reconciliation, pacification, tenderness, goodness, bounty, forgiveness, magnanimity and mercy that Jesus Christ brought us.

We need to have the courage that Paul had when he wrote about himself: "I was once a blasphemer and a persecutor and a violent man" (1 Tim. 1:13). This is how we take the first step toward magnanimity. Because those who only see the speck in the eye of the other end up miserable: petty, small-minded, full of gossip.

THE PATH TO MAGNANIMITY

What does being magnanimous mean? It means having a great heart, having greatness of mind; it means having great ideals, the desire to do great things in response to what God asks of us. For this very reason it is important to do everyday things well: our daily actions, tasks, meetings with people. We need to do the little everyday things with a great heart, open to God and to others.

THE PATH TOWARD PIETY

The gift of piety means being capable of rejoicing with those who rejoice, of weeping with those who weep, of being close to those who are lonely or in anguish, of correcting those in error, of consoling the afflicted, of welcoming and helping those in need. The gift of piety is closely tied to gentleness. The gift of piety which the Holy Spirit gives us makes us gentle, calm, patient, at peace with God, at the service of others with kindness.

THE PATH TOWARD KINDNESS

Consumerist individualism has brought us to great injustice. People are viewed simply as obstacles to our own serene existence. We end up treating them like bothersome annoyances and we become increasingly aggressive. This attitude grows even more accentuated in times of crisis and hardship, when we are tempted to think in terms of "every man for himself." However, even then, we can choose to act with kindness. Those who do are like stars shining in the darkness.

St. Paul describes kindness as a fruit of the Holy Spirit (see Gal. 5:22–3). He uses the Greek word *chrestótes*, which describes an attitude that is gentle, pleasant and supportive, not rude or coarse. Individuals who possess this quality help to make other people's lives more bearable, especially by sharing the weight of their problems, needs and fears. This way of treating others can take different forms: by performing an act of kindness, by not being offended by words or deeds, by showing a readiness to alleviate the other's burdens. It involves "speaking words of comfort, strength, consolation and encouragement" and not "words that demean, sadden, anger or show scorn."[8]

Kindness frees us from the cruelty that at times infects human relationships, from the anxiety that prevents us from thinking of others, from the frantic flurry of activity that forgets that others also have a right to be happy. Often nowadays we find neither the time nor the energy to stop and be kind to others, to say, "Excuse me," "Pardon me," or "Thank you." Yet every now and then, miraculously, a kind person appears, someone who is willing to set everything else aside in order to show interest, to give the gift of a smile, to speak a word of encouragement, to listen amid general indifference.

If we make a daily effort to do precisely this, we can create a healthy social atmosphere in which misunderstandings can be overcome and conflict forestalled. Kindness is not a secondary quality, nor is it a superficial and bourgeois virtue. Precisely because it entails esteem and respect for others, once kindness becomes the culture of a society, it is capable of transforming lifestyles, relationships and the ways ideas are discussed and compared. Kindness facilitates the quest for consensus; it opens new paths where hostility and conflict would burn all bridges.

THE PATH TO PATIENCE

It is not easy to understand what patience is, what it means to be patient in life, what it means to be patient when dealing with challenges. However, we can say that patience is not an attitude that belongs to the vanquished; Christian patience does not belong to the defeated. It is something else entirely.

Patience is a virtue of those who are journeying forward; it does not pertain to those who are closed off and who remain still.

The etymology of the word suggests "carrying," "hoisting upon our shoulders." While a patient person might be tired, they continue to carry the weight, they do not abandon the problem, they do not feel limits, they do not leave behind those who are suffering, they continue to "carry them along" with joy and happiness.

THE PATH TO MEEKNESS

"Blessed are the meek" (Matt 5:5). We, on the other hand, are often impatient, irritable and always ready to complain! We demand so much of others, but when our turn comes, we react by raising our voices, as if we were masters of the world, when in reality we are all children of God.

Instead, let us be like those parents who are so patient with their children even if the little ones "drive them mad." This is the way of the Lord: the way of meekness and patience. Jesus traveled this path: as a child he endured persecution and exile. Then, as an adult, he endured slander, duplicity, false accusations in court. He endured it all with meekness. Out of love for us he endured even the cross.

First keep peace with yourself; then you will be able to bring peace to others. A peaceful man does more good than a learned man. Whereas a passionate man turns even good to evil and is quick to believe evil, the peaceful man, being good himself, turns all things to good. The man who is at perfect ease is never suspicious, but the disturbed and discontented spirit is upset by many a suspicion. He neither rests himself nor permits others to do so. He often says what ought not to be said and leaves undone what ought to be done. He is concerned with the duties of others but neglects his own. Direct your zeal, therefore, first upon yourself; then you may with justice exercise it upon those about you.

Thomas à Kempis[9]

THE FLIGHT AND REST

The Commandment regarding the day of rest (see Gen. 2:3; Exod. 20:8–11) sounds like an easy command to respect, but it is not. True rest is not simple, because there is false rest and true rest. How can we recognize them?

Today's society thirsts for amusement and holidays. The entertainment industry is flourishing, with advertising portraying the ideal world as one great amusement park where everyone has fun. Today, the prevailing concept of *life* does not have its center of gravity in activity and commitment, but in *escapism*. We earn money in order to have fun, to satisfy ourselves. The model before us is that of a successful person who can afford ample room for diverse forms of enjoyment. But this mentality makes a person slip into a dissatisfied life that is anesthetized by fun that is alienating and escapist, not restful. Humankind has never had as many opportunities for rest as it does today, and yet it has never experienced as much emptiness! Opportunities for entertainment, amusement, cruises and travel abound, but these do not bring about a full heart. They do not bring about rest.

What, then, is rest according to this Commandment? It is the moment of contemplation; it is the moment of praise, not of escapism. It is the time to look at reality and say, "How beautiful life is!" Contrary to rest as an escape from reality, the Decalogue (the Ten Commandments) proposes rest as the *blessing of reality*.

For us Christians, the center of the Lord's day, Sunday, is the Eucharist, which means *thanksgiving*. It is the day to say to God, "Thank you, Lord, for life, for your mercy, for all your gifts." Sunday is not the day to forget all the other days but to remember them, bless them and make peace with life. How many people there are who have endless opportunities to amuse themselves, but who are not at peace with life! Sunday is the day to make peace with life and say, "Life is precious." It is not easy; sometimes it is painful, but it is precious.

OUR LIVES ARE A WHITE CANVAS
WAITING FOR COLOR

The Magi traveled to Bethlehem (see Matt. 2:1–11). Their pilgrimage speaks to us, too, as we are also called on to journey toward Jesus, for he is the North Star that lights up the sky of life and guides our steps toward true joy. But where did the Magi's pilgrimage to encounter Jesus begin? What encouraged these men of the East to set out on their journey?

In truth, the Magi had many excellent reasons *not* to leave. They were wise men and astrologers, famous and wealthy. Having attained sufficient cultural, social and economic security, they could have remained content with what they already knew and possessed. Instead, they let themselves be unmoored by a question and a sign: "Where is the one who has been born king of the Jews? We saw his star…" (Matt. 2:2). They did not allow their hearts to retreat into the caves of gloom and apathy; they longed to see the light. They were not content to plod through life; they yearned for new and greater horizons. Their eyes were not fixed here below; they were windows open to the heavens.

Where did this spirit of healthy restlessness originate? It was born of *desire*. That was their secret: the capacity to desire. Let us ponder this. To desire means to fuel the fire that burns within; it drives us to look beyond what is immediate and visible. To desire means embracing life as a great mystery, as if it were a chink in a wall that opens on to distant horizons, accepting that life is not just "here and now" but also "elsewhere." It is like a blank canvas that cries out for color. A great painter, Vincent van Gogh, once said that his need for God drove him to go out at night to paint the stars. For that is the way God made us: brimming with desire, directed, like the Magi, toward the stars.

Without exaggerating, we can say that we are what we desire. For our desires widen our gaze and drive our lives forward, beyond the barriers of habit, beyond banal consumerism, beyond a drab and dreary faith, beyond the fear of becoming involved and serving others and the common good. In the words of St. Augustine, "The whole life of a good Christian is a holy desire."[10]

RESTLESSNESS AND FREEDOM

Freedom makes a person free to the extent that it transforms their life and directs them toward goodness. In order to be truly free, we not only need to know ourselves on a psychological level, but also and above all to practice truth in ourselves on a more profound level. We need to open ourselves to the grace of Christ in our hearts.

Truth should make us restless and disturb us. Let us focus on this extremely Christian word: restlessness. We know that many Christians are never restless: their lives are always the same; there is no movement in their hearts; they lack restlessness.

Why is restlessness important? Because it is a sign that the Holy Spirit is at work in us, that freedom is an active freedom, that it comes from the grace of the Holy Spirit. This is why I say that freedom should make us restless and disturb us; it should constantly lead us to question ourselves so that we might move ever deeper into what and who we really are. In this way we can discover that the journey of truth and freedom is a tiring one, one that lasts a lifetime.

Remaining free is tiring; it is a struggle. But it is not impossible. Take courage, and let us move forward with this; it will be good for us. It is a journey that is guided and sustained by the love that comes from the cross, the love that reveals truth to us and grants us freedom. This is the path to happiness. Freedom can make us free, joyful, happy.

A RIVER OF JOY

The Gospel, radiant with the glory of Christ's cross, constantly invites us to rejoice. A few examples will suffice. "Rejoice!" is the angel's greeting to Mary (Luke 1:28). Mary's visit to Elizabeth makes John jump for joy in his mother's womb (see Luke 1:41). In her song of praise, Mary proclaims, "My spirit rejoices in God my Savior" (Luke 1:47). When Jesus begins his ministry, John cries out, "That joy is mine" (John 3:29). Jesus himself was "full of joy through the Holy Spirit" (Luke 10:21). His message brings us joy: "I have told you this so that my joy may be in you and that your joy may be complete" (John 15:11).

Our Christian joy drinks of the wellspring of his brimming heart. He promises his disciples, "You will weep and mourn while the world rejoices" (John 16:20). He then goes on to say, "But I will see you again and you will rejoice, and no one will take away your joy" (John 16:22). The disciples were "overjoyed" at the sight of the risen Christ (John 20:20).

In the Acts of the Apostles we read that the first Christians "ate together with glad and sincere hearts" (Acts 2:46). Wherever the disciples went, "there was great joy" (Acts 8:8). Even amid persecution they continued to be "filled with joy" (Acts 13:52). The newly baptized eunuch "went on his way rejoicing" (Acts 8:39), while Paul's jailer "was filled with joy because he had come to believe in God—he and his whole household" (Acts 16:34).

What is holding us back from entering this great river of joy, too?

PROFOUND JOY IS A GIFT

When he had led them out to the vicinity of Bethany, he lifted up his hands and blessed them. While he was blessing them, he left them and was taken up into heaven. Then they worshipped him and returned to Jerusalem with great joy. And they stayed continually at the temple, praising God.

(Luke 24:50–53)

But what exactly is this joy? Is it being cheerful? No, that is not the same thing. Cheerfulness is good, but if we want to live it all the time, in the end it gets transformed into lightness and superficiality and can conduct us to a state where Christian wisdom is lacking. Joy is something else, something greater. It is deeper. It is a gift of the Lord who fills us from the inside. It is akin to being anointed by the Holy Spirit.

Joy is knowing that Jesus is both with us and with the Father.

TRUE JOY

True joy does not come from things or from possessions. No! It is born from the encounter, from relationship with others; it is born from feeling accepted, understood and loved; and from accepting, understanding and loving. It is not because of a passing fancy but because the other is a person.

Joy is born from the gratuitousness of an encounter! It is hearing someone say, although not necessarily with words, "You are important to me."

In calling to you, God says, "You are important to me, I love you, I am counting on you." Jesus says this to each of us! Joy comes from that! Understanding and hearing this is the secret of our joy. Feeling loved by God, knowing that, for him, we are not numbers but people; hearing him call us is joy.

A JOY THAT NO ONE CAN EVER TAKE AWAY FROM US

If we remain in him, his joy will remain in us (see John 15:9–11). We will not be sad disciples and bitter apostles. On the contrary, we will reflect on and be heralds of true happiness—that complete joy that no one can take away from us. We will spread the hope of a new life that Christ has given us.

God's call is not a heavy burden that robs us of joy. Sometimes it might feel like a burden, but it never robs us of joy; we feel joy even in its burden. God does not want us to sink into sadness—one of the evil spirits that takes over the soul and is denounced by the Desert Fathers. God does not want us to be weighed down with the sadness and fatigue that come from a life lived poorly, without a spirituality that brings joy to our lives—and even to our weariness. The infectiousness of our joy ought to be the first proof of our closeness with and love for God. When we shine with the joy that comes from an encounter with the Lord, we are true dispensers of God's grace.

TRUE LIFE

How often we have felt the need for a change that would affect our entire person! How often have we said to ourselves, "I need to change; I can't keep on like this. My life is leading nowhere, it will never bear fruit, it's all pointless, I'll never be happy." How often have we had these thoughts! And Jesus, who is nearby, always reaches out to us and says, "Come, come to me. I will do the work: I will change your heart, I will change your life, I will make you happy."

Jesus, who is with us, invites us to change our life. It is he, with the Holy Spirit, who sows in us this restlessness to change our lives and become better people.

Let us accept the Lord's invitation without resistance. Only by opening ourselves to his mercy will we find true life and true joy. All we have to do is open the door—he will do the rest. He does everything; we just have to open our hearts. He can heal us and help us move forward. I assure you that we will all be happier.

Works Cited

St. Augustine, *Epistle 155*
Dante Alighieri, *The Divine Comedy*, tr. H. W. Longfellow
Mario Benedetti, "I Love You," tr. Paul Archer
Robert Hugh Benson, *The Lord of the World*
Francisco Luis Bernárdez, "To Recover," tr. Sarah Salazar
Jorge Luis Borges, "John 1:14," tr. Willis Barnstone
G. K. Chesterton, *The Defendant*
John Donne, "Death be not Proud"
F. M. Dostoevsky, *The Brothers Karamazov*, tr. Constance Garnett
St. Peter Faber, *Memoriale* 30 June 1543
Francis of Assisi, *The Canticle of the Creatures*
St. John of the Cross, "Living Flame of Love"
St. John of the Cross, "The Fountain"
Friedrich Hölderlin, "Meiner verehrungswürdigen Großmutter Zu
    ihrem 72. Geburtstag."
Friedrich Hölderlin, "To Hope," tr. Robert Huddleston
Gerard Manley Hopkins, "God's Grandeur"
St. Ignatius of Loyola, *Rules*
St. Ignatius of Loyola, *Autobiography*
Thomas à Kempis, *Imitation of Christ*
Ethel Mannin, *Late I have Loved Thee*
Alessandro Manzoni, *The Betrothed*
Novalis, Spiritual Chants V, IX, XI
B. L. Pasternak, *Doctor Zhivago*, tr. Hayward and Harari
Octavio Paz, "Brotherhood," tr. Eliot Weinberger
J. R. R. Tolkien, *The Lord of the Rings*
Virgilio, "The Aeneid"

Films Cited

Francesco, giullare di Dio, Directed by Roberto Rossellini, Screenplay by Roberto Rossellini, Federico Fellini, Brunello Rondi, Italy, 1950.

Il pranzo di Babette, Directed by Gabriel Axel, Screenplay by Gabriel Axel, Denmark, 1987.

La strada, Directed by Federico Fellini, Screenplay by Federico Fellini, Tullio Pinelli, Carlo Ponti, Ennio Flaiano, Italy, 1954.

Roma città aperta, Directed by Roberto Rossellini, Screenplay by Sergio Amidei, Federico Fellini, Ferruccio Disnan, Celeste Negarville, Roberto Rossellini, Italy, 1945.

Notes

Fifteen Steps Toward Happiness

1 Augustine of Hippo, "Of True Religion," Book XXXIX, 72
2 Oscar Wilde, *The Picture of Dorian Gray* (first published 1890). Public domain.

Part 1: Happiness Is a Gift We Receive

1 Dante Alighieri, *Divine Comedy*, Paradise, Canto XXXIII 1–21, tr. Henry Wadsworth Longfellow (1807–82). Public domain.
2 Friedrich Hölderlin, "To Hope," translated by Robert Huddleston 2011.
3 Cited by Our Lady of Solitude Monastery, www.desertnuns .com/give-me-your-sins (accessed 4 June 2024).
4 Robert Hugh Benson (1871–1914), *The Lord of the World*. Public domain. www.gutenberg.org/cache/epub/14021/pg14021 .txt (accessed 4 June 2024).
5 Augustine of Hippo, Epistle 155, to Macedonius, in Roland Teske, S.J. (trans.), *Letters: Volume II, Letters 100–155* (New York: New City Press, 2003).
6 *Babette's Feast* (1987), directed by Gabriel Axel.
7 Francisco Luis Bernárdez, "To Recover," translated by Sarah Salazar, theenglishcenterblog.tumblr.com/post/113527898559 /poem-translation (accessed 7 June 2024).

Part 2: Happiness Is a Gift to Be Given

1 "Inunnguiniq IQ Principles," Inuuqatigiit Centre for Inuit Children, Youth and Families, inuuqatigiit.ca/family-well-being -program/parenting-program/inunnguiniq-principles (accessed 7 June 2024).

2 Don Pietro, before being shot by Nazis, in *Rome, Open City* (1945), directed by Roberto Rossellini.

3 "Prayers: Easter Vigil in the Holy Night," iBreviary, www .ibreviary.com/m2/preghiere.php?tipo=Rito&id=544 (accessed 7 June 2024).

4 Fyodor Dostoevsky, *The Brothers Karamazov*, translated by Constance Garnett (New York: The Lowell Press, 2023), Part II, Book 4, Lacerations, Chapter 1, www.gutenberg.org/files/28054 /28054-h/28054-h.htm#book04 (accessed 7 June 2024).

5 "John of the Cross," cited by Our Lady of Mercy Carmelite Community, olmlaycarmelites.org/quote/john-cross?page=1 (accessed 7 June 2024).

6 St. John Chrysostom, *Homiliae in Matthaeum*, 50.3.

7 J. R. R. Tolkien, *The Lord of the Rings: The Two Towers*, HarperCollins ebook, gosafir.com/mag/wp-content/uploads/2019 /12/Tolkien-J.-The-lord-of-the-rings-HarperCollins-ebooks -2010.pdf (accessed 7 June 2024), p. 438.

8 Boris Pasternak, *Doctor Zhivago*, translated by Max Hayward and Manya Harari (New York: Pantheon, 1958), online version at archive.org/stream/DoctorZhivago_201511/Doctor%20Zhivago _djvu.txt (accessed 7 June 2024).

9 St. Ignatius of Loyola: *A Pilgrim's Journey: The Autobiography of Saint Ignatius of Loyola*, jesuits-eum.org/readings/ignatius -autobiography (accessed 7 June 2024).

10 Pope Francis, *Christus Vivit (Christ is Alive): Apostolic Exhortation on Young People* (HijezGlobal, 2019), 76.

11 Pope Francis, *Evangelii Gaudium* (The Joy of the Gospel), 1115.

12 J. R. R. Tolkien, *The Lord of the Rings: The Return of the King*, HarperCollins ebook, gosafir.com/mag/wp-content/uploads /2019/12/Tolkien-J.-The-lord-of-the-rings-HarperCollins -ebooks-2010.pdf (accessed 7 June 2024), p. 879.

Part 3: Happiness Is a Path

1 *Babette's Feast* (1987), directed by Gabriel Axel.
2 Virgil, *The Aeneid*, Book 1, 198–203, translated by John Dryden, www.sparknotes.com/lit/aeneid/full-text/book-i (accessed 7 June 2024).
3 Augustine of Hippo, Sermon 256.
4 St. John of the Cross, "Living Flame of Love," in David Lewis (trans.), *The Living Flame of Love* (London: Thomas Baker, 1919).
5 Dialogue between Il Matto and Gelsomina, *La Strada* (1954), directed by Federico Fellini. This section translated by Oonagh Stransky.
6 Thomas à Kempis, *The Imitation of Christ*, Book III, chapter LIX.
7 John Donne, Holy Sonnet X, "Death, Be Not Proud," www .poetryfoundation.org/poems/44107/holy-sonnets-death-be -not-proud (accessed 10 June 2024). Public domain.

Part 4: Happiness Is Not Just Getting By

1 Gerald Manley Hopkins (1844–89), "God's Grandeur," www .poetryfoundation.org/poems/44395/gods-grandeur (accessed 10 June 2024). Public domain.
2 Thomas à Kempis, *The Imitation of Christ*, Book II, Chapter VI.
3 J. R. R. Tolkien, *The Lord of The Rings: The Fellowship of the Ring*, HarperCollins ebook, gosafir.com/mag/wp-content/uploads /2019/12/Tolkien-J.-The-lord-of-the-rings-HarperCollins-ebooks -2010.pdf (accessed 10 June 2024), pp. 348–9.
4 Father Alberto Hurtado, S.J., "The Obligation of Charity," in *A Fire that Lights other Fires: Selected Pages from Father Alberto Urtado, S.J.*, www.clerus.org/clerus/dati/2012-07/31-13/02_A_Fire .html (accessed 10 June 2024).
5 Jorge Luis Borges, "John 1:14," translated by Willis Barnstone, cited in *Jorge Luis Borges: Selected Poems* (Penguin Modern Classics, 2000).

Part 5: Happiness Is Making Your Dreams Come True

1 Mario Benedetti, "I Love You," translated by Paul Archer, www
.paularcher.net/translations/mario_benedetti/te_quiero.html
(accessed 10 June 2024).

2 St. John of the Cross, "The Fountain," translated by Willis
Barnstone, www.poetry-chaikhana.com/Poets/J/JohnoftheCro
/Fountain/index.html (accessed 10 June 2024).

3 Alessandro Manzoni, *The Betrothed: Volume II, A New
Translation* (London: James Burns, 1844), p. 812.

4 Manzoni, *The Betrothed*, pp. 811–12.

5 Popularly known as "Volare," *Nel blu dipinto di blu* is a famous
Italian song from 1958 about a man who has a dream of being
blue and flying in the sky, inspired by a Chagall painting.

6 G. K. Chesterton, "A Defence of Baby-worship," in *The Defendant*
(Project Gutenberg ebook), www.gutenberg.org/cache/epub/12245
/pg12245-images.html (accessed 10 June 2024).

7 Octavio Paz, "Brotherhood," translated by Eliot Weinberger,
poetrysociety.org/poetry-in-motion/brotherhood-3 (accessed 12
June 2024).

Part 6: Happiness Is Revolutionary

1 Novalis, "Spiritual Chant IX," in George MacDonald, *Exotics: A
Translation of the Spiritual Songs of Novalis, the Hymn-book of
Luther, and Other Poems from the German and Italian* (London:
Strahan and Co, 1876), pp. 22–3.

2 St. Francis of Assisi, "The Canticle of the Creatures" francis
canseculars.com/the-canticle-of-the-creatures (accessed 10 June
2024).

Part 7: Happiness Is Concrete Love

1 Ethel Mannin, *Late Have I Loved Thee: A Novel of Spiritual Regeneration* (New York: Image Books, 1962), p. 240.
2 "Spiritual Chant V," in George MacDonald, *Exotics: A Translation of the Spiritual Songs of Novalis, the Hymn-book of Luther, and Other Poems from the German and Italian* (London: Strahan and Co, 1876), pp. 13–14.
3 St. Ignatius of Loyola, "Rules for perceiving and knowing in some manner the different movements which are caused in the soul," in *The Spiritual Exercises of St. Ignatius of Loyola*, www .documentacatholicaomnia.eu/03d/1491-1556,_Ignatius_ Loyola, Spiritual_Exercises,_EN.pdf (accessed 10 June 2024), p. 68.

Part 8: Happiness a Hundred Times Over in this Life

1 Novalis, extract from "Spiritual Chant XI," in George MacDonald, *Exotics: A Translation of the Spiritual Songs of Novalis, the Hymn-book of Luther, and Other Poems from the German and Italian* (London: Strahan and Co, 1876), p. 28.
2 Augustine of Hippo, *Confessions*, Book X, 27.38.
3 Augustine of Hippo, "Of True Religion," Book XXXIX, 72.
4 J. R. R. Tolkien, *The Lord of The Rings: The Fellowship of the Ring*, HarperCollins ebook, gosafir.com/mag/wp-content/uploads /2019/12/Tolkien-J.-The-lord-of-the-rings-HarperCollins -ebooks-2010.pdf (accessed 10 June 2024), p. 51.
5 Fyodor Dostoevsky, *The Idiot*, first published 1869.
6 "Communication on Progress ACT BEAUTY 2021," United Nations Global Compact, unglobalcompact.org/participation /report/cop/active/469170 (accessed 10 June 2024).
7 Boris Pasternak, *Doctor Zhivago*, translated by Max Hayward and Manya Harari (New York: Pantheon, 1958), online version at archive.org/stream/DoctorZhivago_201511/Doctor%20Zhivago _djvu.txt (accessed 10 June 2024).

NOTES

8 Pope Francis, *Amoris Laetitia*, www.vatican.va/content/dam /francesco/pdf/apost_exhortations/documents/papa-francesco _esortazione-ap_20160319_amoris-laetitia_en.pdf (accessed 10 June 2024), p. 78.

9 Thomas à Kempis, *The Imitation of Christ*, Book II, Chapter III, 1.

10 Augustine of Hippo, "Homily 4 on the First Epistle of John," 6.